Tillie Jamieson

**Tillie Jamieson Chapter 9**
*"Peace in a Severe Storm"*

**Tina Link Chapter 10**
*"Faith Above My Failure"*

Tina Link

Psalm 33:12 New King James Version (NKJV)
12 Blessed is the nation whose God is the Lord,
The people He has chosen as His own inheritance.

America is still a blessed nation and I believe God still has a great plan for us. My heart will always love and honor this land. Being here now for eighty-two years has given me a brief insight into the freedom, pleasures, changes and honor we have given each other as a country who believes and honors the God who loves everyone of us. When we were formed, He had no one else in mind, so each person is special to Him. Do not forget all that has been given and made available to us and we turn our back on Him, well allow me to say it this way. May we never, never risk it!! Though the forces of evil are becoming more and more sinister, there is a corresponding cry for a spiritual awakening, not only in America, but also around the world.

Melinda McGlasson

**Melinda McGlasson Chapter 11**
*"It Isn't about the Struggle, It's about the Victory"*

**Fallon Lee Chapter 12**
*"The Beauty of Ashes"*

Fallon Lee

# "It's Time To"

# Wake Up
# Stand Up
# Look Up

**A LOOK at AMERICA from
the VIEWPOINT of an
ORDINARY AMERICAN CITIZEN**

XULON PRESS ELITE

Xulon Press Elite
2301 Lucien Way #415
Maitland, FL 32751
407.339.4217
www.xulonpress.com

Printed in the United States of America.

Paperback ISBN-13: 978-1-6322-1221-4
eBook ISBN-13: 978-1-6322-1222-1

# DEDICATION

To every true American in this nation who feels like their voice doesn't matter anymore, and you are living out your life in suspense of what's going to happen next in the land we all love, I dedicate this book. The respect and trust have been violated from outside sources and you have received misled information from many people and the media. Your heart for our nation has been damaged, and you are looking for answers now and for the future.

In reality, there is but one person to turn to by faith. We will try to direct your complete trust and allegiance to Him throughout this book. I dedicate these writings also with my deepest love for Him (Jesus Christ). The United States of America and all Americans need the hope He and His Word (the Bible) can give us for the future. There will always be leadership in Washington D.C. we will not agree with their policies, agenda, or just the person they are. There are some things going on in our nation today that only God can bring healing to. If you have noticed in the papers and on television all that is happening in America, then I am sure your heart has been stirred. We address how we all can help in the restoration process throughout this book. As we pray, help is on the way.

May your life and future decisions be made with much prayer and concern for the millions of Americans who will be affected; our hearts cry to the Lord Jesus Christ.

A nation's success depends upon believers in Jesus Christ who believe, rely, and act on the Word of God as explained in the Bible. When a nation looks at God as its leader, the nation will succeed. Psalm 33:12 states: "Blessed is the nation whose God is the Lord, the people He has chosen as His own inheritance."

# ACKNOWLEDGMENTS

S tarting in 1996, traveling across many cities and towns in America, my wife Tillie and I were holding patriotic rallies to help restore patriotism to our nation, and honoring our military veterans as well as those in service at the time. We also proclaimed the "Message to America," which is the Word of God, the Bible. The hours we spent on the road were worth every mile as we saw many of our veterans touched by the Holy Spirit to bring healing and restoration to their lives.

Being a veteran myself gave me a heart for these men and women who had been involved in preserving America's freedom and safety, some for many years of service, in several countries of the world. Some had been hardened in their hearts as a result of all they had seen on the battlefield and kept this inside, but the Holy Spirit knew all about the pain they were carrying, and we saw many with tears in their eyes become set free from those hurts as God touched them.

We would like to acknowledge all of America's military people in every branch of service for their contribution, which includes all of those who paid the ultimate sacrifice of their lives for freedom, and also those living among us in every city and town in this nation, and those on active duty now across the world. "THANKS, VETERANS." We honor you with this book to call all Americans to wake up, stand up, and look up. God bless you today and forever for all you have done.

We would also like to acknowledge and honor all of the family members who stayed at home, supported, and prayed for their sons and daughters while they were away.

Those of you who lost a loved one in battle, our hearts go out to you, and we will always honor their memory with you, the best we know how. May God bless you today and forever is our prayer. "THANKS, FAMILIES."

## THIS PAGE IS ADDED TO ACKNOWLEDGE AND HONOR MANY PEOPLE

When this manuscript was about complete, I became ill for about two months and had to put this aside as America and the world was attacked by the invisible enemy called the coronavirus. This has been very devastating to so many people in our nation. We have prayed and believed for healing to come in a supernatural way, as well as the use of all the available resources known and being developed. The news media has covered this widely across every spectrum available; searching for answers, and what can be done to help all the people affected in so many ways.

We want to use this page to acknowledge, thank, and honor all of the first responders, including the doctors, nurses, firefighters, police, ambulance personnel, food providers, governors, all state officials, pastors, and individual volunteers. We also thank the President, the Vice President, and the task forces who were assembled to carry a very heavy load of decision-making at the critical desperate time needed. There are so many more people working behind the scenes to serve our people, and we thank you for all you have done and are doing every day. God bless you all!

To all of you who have had sick family members or lost your loved ones to this terrible virus, our hearts truly do go out to you, and we continue to pray for healing of all the pain you are experiencing and will continue to have in the future. We bind together with you with cords that cannot be broken because of our love for each other, not only as Americans, but the people God created and loves.

As you read this, may the power of the Holy Spirit touch you all, and may you sense His presence deep where your pain is. God loves you and so do we!!

# TABLE OF CONTENTS

# A Personal Message From Jim Jamieson

As I was leaving home to go to the office and driving down the main street area of our town and looking around at all of the stores, shops, car lots, restaurants, and other businesses, the thought came to me of how blessed we are to live in this peaceful place in America.

The feeling of winter was in the air, and very few cars on the road, but there were several pickup trucks at a local restaurant where farmers and other workers would go for their early morning coffee and breakfast. It was a special place where the conversations would be about politics, the weather, sports, and other topics that would be on the instant agenda.

Life, in general, is going good for most of the people in this Oklahoma town, where there is still a great heart for caring about your neighbor and being helpful when a need becomes known. Arriving at the church where my office is,

I could sense the presence of the Lord on this day to give directions for me personally as this book was destined to become a reality to help the people see the larger picture of our nation at a strategic time.

Most of us have received so much good from living in America, and have had decent lives that brought so much joy and happiness to ourselves and families. Also, I know many have not been so fortunate and struggle for their very existence. We do not know all of the reasons for what we would call injustice in our society. Many agencies and news programs are trying to figure out what can be done about many of the social issues in our nation. When there is a tragedy or disaster, you can see the very heart of this nation as we bind together to lend a helping hand to those in need.

Living in this nation all of my life has been one of the greatest things a person could have ever hoped for. Being raised on a cotton farm in West Texas in the 1940s and the 1950s, to me, was a very hard time, but as I look back on those days, I take great pride in the simple life that became my personal foundation to grow up on. We knew we lived a meager existence, but it didn't matter because there were chores, farm work, love, respect, and happiness all over the place most of the time. So many other farm families were also struggling, and I can still vividly recall those times when we would get together with some of them and have an "ice cream social." I can still hear the laughter, stories, the taste of the ice cream, and cake. We played outside games, and just enjoyed the life we had; so simple, but great.

Writing this from the viewpoint of an ordinary American citizen will be an honor. The reason I chose this phrase is because we are the majority who make up the population of our great country; the hard-working loyal people willing to make sacrifices to support and keep America strong are to be honored and respected. We are the ones crying out for good, common sense, and a love for God to be restored in the lives of everyone. As we believe for an outpouring of the Holy Spirit and the power of God to bring an authentic transformation in hearts, from the White House to my home, and every home in America, then we will see the love for each other become a reality, and our nation become bound together for the future destiny.

Our children, grandchildren, and great-grandchildren deserve the right to live in a great America, as most of us have. There have been many who sacrificed their lives so this could be a reality for the generations who would follow. We should be thankful every day for them and not take the future for granted.

As we take the next steps forward together, my prayer is this book will help us all in the journey towards the restoration of a great nation and each individual person. We will be called on to help in many different ways. It will be worth it all.

# INTRODUCTION

We are living in very critical times in America right now, and it is our desire to share with you our calling to help and do all we can to bring restoration and healing; not only in our nation, but also to each person who is reaching out for directions in their individual life as an American. We want to emphasize the importance of the name of this book. We as the people need to "Wake Up, Stand Up, and Look Up," and do the individual calling in our neighborhood, church, town, city, and vocation where we can <u>reach out, rescue, restore,</u> and <u>repair</u> all that has been torn down or is in the process of being destroyed. We can do it with God's power, and be willing to go the extra mile in many cases.

You might ask as you read, what and how can I help in this enormous need and undertaking? Here are several ways you can be involved and be responsible to complete:

## OPERATION MOBILIZATION

Our Mission is: To <u>enlist</u>, <u>inform</u>, and <u>mobilize</u> American Christians and American citizens regarding the critical and urgent issues that will impact them and the families of this nation for generations to come (remember this: YOU ARE NEEDED NOW).

*I will register and exercise my right to vote in future elections.

*I will pray faithfully for a spiritual awakening to come to all of America.

*I will support the restoration of prayer in America's public schools and events.

*I will become well informed about issues that affect the morality of our nation.

*I will pray for the President and the other leaders of our nation.

*I will do all that I can as an American citizen to make sure that we remain "one nation under God," according to our Pledge of Allegiance.

*I will "stand firm" in my biblical convictions, and will stand for the return of the Ten Commandments and religious freedom.

The great 18th-century British statesman and political thinker Edmund Burke said,

> *"All that is necessary for the triumph of evil is for good men to do nothing."*

# Section One

*It's Time to Wake Up, Stand Up, Look Up*

# WAKE UP

Romans 13:11 New King James Version (NKJV)

Put on Christ

"And do this, knowing the time, that now it is high time to awake out of sleep; for now, our salvation is nearer than when we first believed."

*Chapter 1*

# WHAT WILL IT TAKE?

Matthew 26:40-41 New King James Version (NKJV)

"Then He came to the disciples and found them sleeping, and said to Peter, 'What! Could you not watch with Me one hour? Watch and pray, lest you enter into temptation. The spirit indeed is willing, but the flesh is weak.'"

B efore we take a good view of the Scripture above, I would like to share with you some ordinary thoughts about the title of this chapter. What will it take to wake us up to make preparations for the future events we will face very soon? No person in America wants to hear or read about things that could be doom and gloom or negative. We have been programmed to desire only the positive and the good things in life, and we naturally seek to be around those who teach and preach the feel-good lessons or all that could make my life better. Let me be one to tell you there is absolutely nothing wrong with desiring the best for you and your family's life. God certainly desires to bless you, but He also wants us to be watchful for the things which could affect our spiritual lives. Our enemy would like to take us off track and render us ineffective for the kingdom of God and all that Jesus Christ gave His life for. When He was on the Cross, you were on His mind. Think about that.

There are definitely several wake-up calls going on around us, and no one on this earth can fix all of the problems that exist now. Did you ever think you would be seeing some of the things that are now portrayed openly right before our eyes? Can you even dare to imagine all the future might hold for our children, grandchildren, and great-grandchildren? Many of us have experienced the best America has to offer, and are never satisfied and want more. Maybe it isn't all bad, but the attitudes sometimes display greed, selfishness, and "it's all about me." The I, me, and my syndrome is here in our nation, and there is not much we can do about other people, but we can surely do some work on ourselves and pray for others in this great country we call home.

I absolutely love America, and after 82 years living here, I will not change my mind or heart about the very hard times and the blessed times we have been given as the valleys and the mountain tops have caused us to grow and mature as

Americans. Sharing with you these writings is difficult in many ways because of the mandate to tell you straightforward the things which could help in our time to wake up and seek the truth about our individual lives and the life of our great nation. So much more to share with you later in other chapters.

In the Scripture, we see where Jesus, along with His disciples, was going to the Garden of Gethsemane, and He told them to sit here while He went further to a place to pray. He took with Him Peter and the two sons of Zebedee, James and John. Jesus was very sorrowful and deeply distressed with all that He was dealing with in His heart and the need to be alone to talk to the Father. He told the three disciples to stay in a certain place and keep watch with Him as He went a little further, and there He fell on His face and prayed with intensity about all that was about to happen, not only in His life but the lives of everyone for generations to come. During His prayers, with the pressure on Him, His sweat became as drops of blood.

He got up after a time to go and talk to the three disciples who were there to keep watch with Him, but guess what, He found them asleep and He said "What! Could you not watch with Me one hour?" In the modern tone, it could have sounded like this: Wake up, you have been with me over three years, and I have asked very little from you, but now

I need you, my friends, to be with Me; please stay awake and watch.

Jesus went back to pray and be alone with the Father, and this time, He asked for the cup He was about to take to be taken away, but He said in His prayer, "Father, Your will be done." He got up and went back to see and maybe talk with His friends, but He found them asleep again because their eyes were heavy. He went back to pray some more.

After the third time, He came back and they were sleeping, and He told them to rise, "let us be going for the hour is at hand, and the Son of Man is being betrayed into the hands of sinners. See, my betrayer is at hand." Jesus had a need during the time at Gethsemane. He was still in human flesh, and His desire was for His disciples to stay awake and just be there, watching with Him. Was this request too much to ask?

As I read over this Scripture, my thoughts went back to when I was pastoring or traveling as an evangelist and saw with my own eyes how many people in the churches were sleeping. They were awake during the singing and other parts of the service, but when it came time for the preaching, they would look at their watches and soon dozed off to sleep and woke up periodically, but would go back to sleep, until their wives punched them in the ribs with an elbow. The scene was kind of funny at times, and on the way out the door, some would tell you how much they enjoyed the sermon.

America needs some watchmen (men and women) to be awake in their spirit and heart, and give guidance for others as we bind together to see our homeland become a strong tower of light again. With the Holy Spirit working in the lives of those who are willing to be on the front lines of healing and restoration of this nation, we might believe together for a great spiritual awakening to come. May it be done to the glory of God! Americans, wake up and look around, see your place where you can be an influence for change for now and future generations.

I am sharing a personal story with you about my best friend from grade school and the rest of our school terms in Littlefield, Texas. For the sake of identity, I will call him by his nickname, Babe. He was a one-of-a-kind friend, lasting a lifetime, and we became almost close as brothers; we spent so much time together. In those great days called the 50s, we would spend time in our cars dragging Main Street, and chasing the girls, or just having an exciting time driving around. That was the thing to do for almost all school kids, honking our horns at each other, hanging out the windows, and just plain acting crazy. On Saturday night, Main Street was bumper-to-bumper cruising, changing cars, and riding around with other friends to save gasoline. Gasoline was expensive in those days; sometimes we had to pay 25 cents a gallon. We still call them the good ole days, and they were.

Many times, Babe would ask me to spend the night at his home, which was not unusual in those days. He had the neatest parents, and I really enjoyed my time there. Everybody's mother was an awesome cook, and she could make the best breakfasts you ever ate. Babe and I were in high school at that time, so we could eat and eat. It was like we had hollow legs as much as we could put away (great memories).

Babe was very hard to wake up in the mornings. So this is where the story gets interesting. Every morning, his mother would come in about 7:00 and say to him: "Babe, it's time to get up," and he would just grunt, and she would turn and walk out. 10 minutes later, she would come back, and with more authority in her voice, she would say: "Babe, I told you it's time to get up, so get up, now." He would say something like, "go on and leave me alone and I'll get up soon." She would turn and walk out again, and guess what? Ten minutes later, she would come back, and Babe was still asleep. This time, it became entertaining for me because I was awake the first time she came in. Here is what happened next:

She would pull the covers from his bare shoulder and start slapping it very hard and would be laughing all the time she was hitting him. After a few of those hard slaps, Babe would tell her to get out of the room and leave him alone, but guess what? He was up, standing on his feet, fully awake, and ready for battle. His mother just turned and went toward the kitchen and was laughing all the way. Babe's mother won the battle, and Babe was up mumbling something, but was there to get ready for the day! This was better than a circus!

*Chapter 2*

# THE TIME CLOCK IS TICKING

Ephesians 5:14-17 New King James Version
(NKJV)

"Therefore He says: 'Awake, you who sleep,
Arise from the dead, And Christ will give you
light.' See then that you walk circumspectly,
not as fools but as wise, redeeming the time,
because the days are evil. Therefore do not
be unwise, but understand what the will of
the Lord is."

M aking a wrong decision that could impact you and
your family's life for the future seems to be something almost everyone has done. Over the years in talking
with many people, the stories of miscalculations have
played a part of a failure in their lives. This is the statement,
which is communicated, "If I had only done what I knew

was the right thing to do, our lives would had been so different. I didn't do it, and missed out financially and in many other ways. I had to deal with the guilt of being unwilling to take the chance or the opportunity given to me. I was either unwise, lazy, fearful, or mentally asleep to seize the open door for a wonderful situation." This sounds so true for many of us, including myself, and maybe you as well. I will tell you a story given me of a missed financial opportunity several years ago.

We had a great friend who was a super Christian businessman. We went to the same church, and spent time at their home on many occasions and had great fellowship together; such a kindhearted person with great integrity and business values. I really respected him in every way, and enjoyed spending time together. He was the president of a large freight-trucking firm, which delivered packages of all kinds in the Dallas, Texas area.

He came to me one day while we were having an evening meal at a restaurant, and he wanted to talk specifically to me about an opportunity. He was a quiet man, and he told me he knew of a situation, which could change our lives financially in a big way. He said his involvement could really change his personal financial picture. He told me about an individual who was getting shipments of supplies to the trucking firm he was the president of, and the person did not have the money to pay the freight bills for all of his parts and things he needed for his new business. He and the individual negotiated a way he could share and charge in the person's new company to pay for the freight bills. This evidently went on for some time until the company was able to take care of his financial obligations. My friend took a risk, and it really paid off for him over time.

He asked me if I could get some resources together to invest in this new company and buy interest at a very low price. This sounded like a great opportunity, but I would have had to go to a bank at the time to get a loan to make the investment. This was a time when there were so many multiple-level marketing schemes being offered to everyone to get in on the ground floor, and you could get rich if you bought into it. I had seen the failures of so many of those deals, and my friends had lost their initial investments in those so-called great deals.

I had never bought interest in anything before, and the fear came over me that I would be making the wrong decision and couldn't afford to lose any money at this time. So I made an unwise calculation without praying or thinking about this any further. To make this story shorter, the company turned out to be a national company, as this became an internationally recognized organization. My friend became very wealthy because of the risk he took, and I stayed the same. I was proud for him and his family. Do I have guilt over this, and I can say no because God still had a great plan for our lives, and we are still living it? We are rich in His love and all He has made available, and we are very thankful for these benefits.

The Scripture we started this chapter with can make so many applications to our lives, so together, let's explore all Paul is communicating to the saints at Ephesus in this Scripture. There are several points we can share which might help you understand where we are as a people and as a nation, and all we need to consider helping bring the changes we need. The title of this chapter is "The Time Clock is Ticking," and there is so much work to be done, and we are not for sure of the timetable we have, but let's get busy as dedicated Americans.

Four points we need to talk about from the book of Ephesians are as follows: *Walk in Unity*, *Walk in Love*, *Walk in Light*, and *Walk in Wisdom*. Each of these points could take some time to share, and we will talk briefly about them as we go along.

**1. Walk in Unity:** As we see our nation being torn apart in so many ways, we as a people who really care about the future of America must do our best to bind together, and walk with a great purpose of restoration and healing. Paul said, "With all lowliness and gentleness, with longsuffering, bearing with one another in love, endeavoring to keep the unity of the Spirit in the bond of peace" (Ephesians 4:2-3).

We make applications with these two verses for us to know we have the power in Christ to walk, talk, and bring unity wherever we go in the marketplace or in our workplace. No, it is not going to be easy in most cases, even in families, but we have the Holy Spirit to bring about the power encounters when needed, and there is an open door for unity. Prayer is the most essential thing to open doors and being willing to walk forward without fear.

**2. Walk in Love:** "Therefore be imitators of God as dear children. And walk in love, as Christ also has loved us and given Himself for us, an offering and a sacrifice to God for a sweet-smelling aroma" (Ephesians 5:1-2). Have you ever been around people who never showed love to others or family members? Those who have received Christ into their hearts have a never-ending love in their hearts God has given them. It is not a love to manipulate, but it is a heart-felt love you can't wait to demonstrate to others. We live in a time in America where it is very difficult to love or care for some people who are bringing division in our nation, and are seemingly out to destroy those that have sacrificed their lives. What can we do about our attitudes in many negative situations like this? When Jesus was on the Cross, He demonstrated His love to all the people of the world. The Scripture says the days are evil, and we are to be wise and do what the will of the Lord is. We are to walk in love as He did when He walked the earth. Very few will choose this course of action. Will you?

**3. Walk in Light:** I feel the need to post the following Scriptures in Chapter 5 of Ephesians.

> "[8]For you were once darkness, but now you are light in the Lord. Walk as children of light [9] (for the fruit of the Spirit *is* in all goodness, righteousness, and truth), [10] finding out what is acceptable to the Lord. [11] And have no fellowship with the unfruitful works of darkness, but rather expose them. [12] For it is shameful even to speak of those things which are done by them in secret. [13] But all things that are [exposed are made manifest by the light, for whatever makes manifest is light."

The Scripture we used at the start of the chapter says: "Awake, you who sleep, arise from the dead, And Christ will give you light." When it talks about "arise from the dead," it is talking about rising up from laziness. We have made mention of the people in America who are sleeping, so to speak, as the situations around us get more critical and believe this will all pass away, and everything will be alright without their involvement or working to help solve some of the issues. Recently, the news said 54% of the Christians did not even vote in the last election. Can you imagine the changes we could see if all of the 164 million people who say they are followers of Christ would become involved and even vote? This is about 65% of the population, and has decreased from 81% in 2001.

As darkness comes, the light of God's people can turn on their lights and let them shine to dispel much of the darkness invading our land. I am not being negative, but looking through the eyes of the Word of God and seeing some of the happening right before us, we are destined to do something. Each of our gifts God has given us can help in so many ways, and we must redeem the time and all that has been stolen from us.

When I sleep at night, I have a night light on in several places in our home, in case I need to get up for some reason. Those little lights dispel some of the darkness, and I can see where I am going and not stumble or fall down and hurt myself. When I used to travel, there was always a light for me in an unfamiliar place so I could see and not be lost in a strange place. The Christian's light needs to come on very brightly to show the people around the USA the importance of the light of Christ to help bring them out of the dark areas of their lives as they are looking for help. The time clock is ticking.

**4. Walk in Wisdom:** Please read this Scripture about walking in wisdom.

Ephesians 5:15-21 New King James Version (NKJV)

"See then that you walk circumspectly, not as fools but as wise, [16] redeeming the time, because the days are evil. Therefore do not be unwise, but understand what the will of the Lord *is.* And do not be drunk with wine, in which is dissipation; but be filled with the Spirit, speaking to one another in psalms and hymns and spiritual songs, singing and making melody in your heart to the Lord, giving thanks always for all things to God the Father in the name of our Lord Jesus Christ, submitting to one another in the fear of God."

As we do our best to mobilize Christians and Americans to help bring our nation back to a place where the generations who follow us will have a great place to live and enjoy as we have. We have to depend on God and use wisdom as we elect those people who will be working for us in Washington D.C. as our leaders. We never really know how they are going to turn out when they have been elected and been in that environment for a while, even when we pray for them. The time clock is ticking and time is passing so fast, so we have to be very wise and use wisdom in our own lives and the love for our country.

*Chapter 3*

# WHERE IS YOUR INTEREST?

(good question)

Acts 20:7-12 New King James Version (NKJV)

Paul Ministering at Troas

"Now on the first *day* of the week, when the disciples came together to break bread, Paul, ready to depart the next day, spoke to them and continued his message until midnight. There were many lamps in the upper room where they were gathered together. And in a window sat a certain young man named Eutychus, who was sinking into a deep sleep. He was overcome by sleep; and as Paul continued speaking, he fell down from the third story and was taken up dead. But Paul went

down, fell on him, and embracing *him* said,
'Do not trouble yourselves, for his life is in
him.' Now when he had come up, had broken
bread and eaten, and talked a long while, even
till daybreak, he departed. And they brought
the young man in alive, and they were not a
little comforted."

The old phrase comes to mind: "Help, I've fallen, and I can't get up!" Most of the ministers, preachers, and evangelists in our nation are trying very, very hard to get people to wake up because the message is the return of Jesus Christ could be very soon. It seems very difficult to get the interest in lives to a level of understanding the urgency of the time or hour. Not to place condemnation on any person, but the heartfelt message is becoming more intense as time passes each day. As we take a panoramic view of America, we can make our own assessment of the situation as our nation is losing its way in the spiritual mindset. We are taking for granted we are a Christian nation, because we recite the Pledge of Allegiance and say together, "one nation under God." Are we really a Christian nation? Just a question that came to me as I was writing. Do we truly honor God and live for Him the way we should or the way we have been taught?

I would like to tell you a story I heard some time ago, and I'm not sure it is true, but maybe there is a point to the story. There was this traveling evangelist who was a very good speaker and had tremendous success every time in his meetings. On this one particular evening, he preached a dynamic sermon about people giving their hearts and lives to Jesus Christ as their Lord and Savior. With sweat on his forehead and handkerchief in one hand, the Bible in the other, he was really shouting it out. He always expected to have a great altar call with people being healed, repenting of their sins, being delivered from all kinds of bondage, and the start of a great revival after his preaching. He had the congregation bow their heads, and he bowed his also, and told people, those who wanted to ask Jesus Christ into their hearts, to come forward and meet him at the altar.

He paused for a minute or two, with expectations of several or many to come forward from the large crowd. He peeked through his fingers and saw no one had come forward, so he changed his appeal to anyone who wanted to receive deliverance from any habit in their lives to please come forward, now. He waited and again peeked through his fingers and saw no one had made a move towards the altar. He was becoming very frustrated because this had never happened to him before, and he was embarrassed about the situation. To make a longer story short, out of desperation, he made this very forceful appeal, "If you love your mother, please come forward now!" He finally got many people to come and stand in front of him, waiting on what to do next. Service was over!

The question is, where is your interest? Is it to become involved in the solutions or the problems our nation has right now? Let me tell you, at this point, there are plenty of problems to go around which need addressing, and each one is very important to some or many people. My heart is touched when I see young people doing so many great things to help in the solutions for other Americans. The news channels usually do not address the good being done, but focus on the problems, and try to use it as leverage for promotions or election purposes. Local radio and tv stations are very good about telling and showing servant Americans in action around their viewing areas. I am proud of them for their hearts to show the good going on. We have students in schools who are touching, helping, and giving of themselves in an organized way to relieve the pain and stress of others in need. God is blessing our nation in this way. Keep up the good work, all of you.

Now, let's take a look at the Scripture reference at the beginning of this chapter. As you can see, Paul was with the disciples at Troas and was going to leave the next day. So he began ministering to all in attendance. Paul was long-winded that evening, and he continued his message until midnight because he had so much to share with them. There were lights in different places so people could see as he was positioned where everyone could hear, even to the third story.

There was a young man, named Eutychus (meaning, "fortunate"), sitting in a window on the third story of the building,
and as Paul preached on and it was getting later, the young
man became very sleepy and was on the edge of the window,
and he went into a deep sleep, and he fell down from his
place and was taken for dead. Evidently in the urgent situation, Paul left his preaching, and went down and fell on
the boy and embraced him, and he told the others not to
trouble themselves, for life was still in him. A miracle took
place that evening, and when Paul had come up, had broken
bread, eaten, and talked a long while, even until daybreak,
he then left, got on a ship from Troas, and went to Miletus.
Paul was a very busy man, carrying the message of Jesus
Christ around the world. The Bible says they brought the
young man in alive.

Several applications can be drawn from the passage. First,
you determine your interest and learn from Eutychus to stay
awake, learn, and be very careful of your position during the
process of getting educated by someone like Paul. Every situation is an education in some way. I call it the University
of Self-Discovery. Maybe you need the power of the Holy
Spirit in your life to help out when there is a need. When
there is a crisis, you can be there to help someone who
gets sleepy in life. They are everywhere, and crying out for
prayer, love, acceptance, forgiveness, and hope. Find your
area of interest in helping restore America in every way
possible as we work together.

# Chapter 4

# STORMS ARE ON THE WAY

L iving in the Oklahoma Panhandle has brought to mind some very vivid times from the past as the pioneers settled here so many years ago. Some of them endured some very difficult situations as the Dust Bowl days of the 1930s came. Many families were forced to move to other parts of the nation, but some stayed and weathered the harsh and painful days and nights, which had to be terrible. The dust was all over everything, inside of the houses, and outside several feet deep. I deeply admire those pioneers, the ones who left, and those staying behind and enduring what had to be a nightmare life for several years.

The roots of those tough people went deep as they stood the test of time with the storms coming very regular. One particular day was called Black Friday as the wall cloud of dirt, and everything it picked up along the way could be seen for miles. People tried to run for cover to a safe place, as many believed this could be the end of the world. The available pictures that were taken at the time can almost prove their point.

Being raised in the West Texas town of Littlefield Texas, even later than the Dust Bowl days, we would have terrible sand-storms, which could last for two or three days. In our farm home, we would wake up in the mornings, covered in the fine dust. This accumulation would have to be swept and shoveled from the linoleum floors of the morning. These were very hard times on my mom and dad as there was a constant struggle to try and get a crop from the fields and garden to supply our food needs. I guess everyone in those days had to be tough, and we just thought this was all a part of life.

The reason I share these stories with you is that as the different kinds of storms approach our America and even around the world, we are going to have to put down some strong roots. To be able to endure the things which are already happening and are going to come very soon, we cannot be weak-minded, but we must know who we are as Americans, and put our faith and trust in God and His Word. We are living in a time when we just do not know what is going to happen next. What we are going to tell you is not to frighten or put a negative cloud on your life, but to help in the way of preparation and knowledge so you can endure and stand firm in the storms.

Another illustration came to my mind, and it is about trees. I have had the privilege to travel in so many states and cities in the USA, and different countries of the world, and many of them have too many trees. I call it unequal distribution as our area is not overwhelmed with a lot of trees, but we certainly love every tree we have been blessed with. Most of the trees by the river have died because the water table became so low, and their roots were not deep enough to sustain their life. When we moved here in 1964 and after, it was a beautiful sight to go down by the river and have a family picnic. The banks of the river were lined with trees as far as you could see, and the water was running so our kids could get their feet wet. Today, the sight is now barren of those beautiful tall trees, which gave so much joy to the people living in this area. The river very seldom has any water in it, except when we get blessed with a large rainfall.

Driving around our city, I saw some old, old, tall stately trees blowing in the almost constant winds we have, and you could see some of their roots on top of the ground, but there was no telling just how deep those roots must be as they constantly seek after water and nutrients to sustain their life for maybe a hundred years or so, who knows for sure? Those trees are very special as they have endured so much, and their anchor is deep, and they seem to just grow stronger, and they have a story to tell with their lives, but probably no one has the time to stop, look, and listen. I am not advocating everyone go out and talk to a tree, but we might pause and look.

At this point, allow me to ask a question or two. What happens to you when the storms or winds of adversity blow in your life? Are your roots down deep in God and His Word, where you will not be toppled over or flattened, or do you grow stronger during and after such adversity or storms in life? This Scripture speaks volumes to all of our hearts.

### Colossians 2:6-7

"As you therefore have received Christ Jesus the Lord, so walk in Him, rooted and built up in Him and established in the faith, as you have been taught, abounding in it with thanksgiving."

For the balance of this chapter about "Wake Up: Storms Are on the Way," the desire is to become very serious about our future as a nation, and a Scripture from the Bible. Please open your minds and hearts to receive these words. Ponder them and study each verse, so we can help others prepare for the future and keep living a life which is pleasing to the Lord. I ask for the Holy Spirit to illuminate the words as you read them, and bring application to everyone who reads this book, for the glory of God.

Matthew 24:4-13 New King James Version (NKJV)

"And Jesus answered and said to them: "Take heed that no one deceives you. For many will come in My name, saying, 'I am the Christ,' and will deceive many. And you will hear of wars and rumors of wars. See that you are not troubled; for all these things must come to pass, but the end is not yet. For nation will rise against nation, and kingdom against kingdom. And there will be famines, pestilences, and earthquakes in various places. All these are the beginning of sorrows."

"Then they will deliver you up to tribulation and kill you, and you will be hated by all nations for My name's sake. And then many will be offended, will betray one another, and will hate one another. Then many false prophets will rise up and deceive many. And because lawlessness will abound, the love of many will grow cold. But he who endures to the end shall be saved."

In this Scripture, the disciples came to Jesus privately as He sat on the Mount of Olives, and they were saying to Him, "Tell us when these certain things will be and what will be the sign of Your coming, and the end of the age?" They were becoming very inquisitive about this, just as we are today. We might be enjoying this life so much, we cannot accept the fact there is an eternity, but certain things must come to pass before we might see the return of Jesus Christ, and no one knows for sure, except the Father in Heaven.

I am not a prophet or a teacher of prophecy, but we have the Word of God, His written Word that is a road map of events that will take place. There is becoming a belief in many churches and Christian circles; we are getting closer and closer as things around the world are happening at a more rapid pace. We are warned to not be deceived by anyone, but stay in His Word and be faithful to His leadership. The Bibles says, "My sheep hear my voice, and I know them, and they follow Me" (John 10:27). Remember to read His Word and listen to His voice, and He will direct your paths in life.

I am very concerned about the storms in Washington and our nation's Capitol right now, and this could be an ongoing problem in America for years to come. Americans fighting Americans and our leadership can't fight for our causes because of the internal battles, which exist like never before; Democrats against Republicans, and the other way around, at times. When elections come up in the future, there could be marching and violence in the streets, and family members turning against each other because of what they see and believe. Are we completely losing our way as "one nation under God," or are we giving credence to the enemy who would like to see us destroyed by fighting with each other? In my personal family, there are Democrats, Republicans, Independents, and whatever they want to be, but my hope and prayer is that the family blood that runs through our veins is much thicker than the political position we would each take as our right might be. We should not be divided or quit having anything to do with a family member because of a political party affiliation, unless they have gone off of the deep end to cause others harm.

May our love for each other prevail over issues that will not last for eternity. We cannot fight all of the battles or storms that exist, but we can have an opinion and common sense in the way to handle our disagreements in a sensible way. We all need to bind together and believe God will help, and we can see America become united and strong again, pulling together. Sometimes we need to come apart before we come apart! The first "come apart" is to come apart and pray for all Americans and America. We need to become involved in the solutions instead of the problems. Wake up America!!

# Section Two

## *It's Time to Wake Up, Stand Up, Look Up*

# STAND UP

**Put on Christ**

Proverbs 14:34 New King James Version (NKJV)

"Righteousness exalts a nation, but sin *is* a reproach to *any* people."

## Chapter 5

# Standing Up When the House Is Divided

Mark 3:23-27 New King James Version (NKJV)

" So He called them to *Himself* and said to them in parables: 'How can Satan cast out Satan? If a kingdom is divided against itself, that kingdom cannot stand. And if a house is divided against itself, that house cannot stand. And if Satan has risen up against himself, and is divided, he cannot stand, but has an end. No one can enter a strong man's house and plunder his goods, unless he first binds the strong man. And then he will plunder his house.'"

I recently got the post in the next paragraph on Messenger, and I knew right away it was going to fit in with some of the topics we are writing about in this chapter. The person who sent this to me is a great American Christian lady, and she has her opinion about some of the things going on right now across our nation. She, just like any of us, has the right to speak and share her heart out of love for God and country. This goes very well with the Scripture we shared above.

*Your post about the current state of America brings this to mind: "A house divided against itself cannot stand." There are those who would go so far as to tear down this nation's foundation in order to rebuild it according to their own ideology. The devil comes to steal, kill, & destroy. If our "house" is destroyed, we become like vagabonds. Without a home. The book "The Man Without a Country" comes to mind. I need to read it again. If I recall, it's about a man who learns to love his country after it was too late. Let's pray that doesn't happen to America. I do not understand how Americans can have so much hatred toward their country unless it's because God has given them over to a reprobate mind.*

She also had the following post, *"Contrary to what some would have us believe, we are a Christian nation. And if we who are called by His name, will seek His face, He will hear our prayers & heal our land. Where two or three are gathered together in His name, He is in the midst of them. Let us pray in one accord, without ceasing. Not just for America, but for all who are in need of a savior. And in everything, give thanks and let all glory be to God alone."*

It is so good to hear from other Americans who are also very concerned about the things going on, not only in our Capitol, but across so many cities all around us. I saw the title of a book recently, and the front cover stood out to me, as it said, "America on the Edge," is it too late to turn back? As we take a stand when there is so much division, we ask ourselves, what are we to do? Well, with the help of God, we can do something very significant as we bind together and link arm in arm, and stand firm and do some responsible things. Let's face it; we live in a nation now filled with turmoil and change. Just about all of the standards of godly conduct are changing or under attack now. It is so difficult to write about all of these matters without getting upset or angry because we have lived in a time in America a few years ago when there wasn't the division we see and hear about now.

In our spiritual lives, we have the Bible as a reference to guide us on our journey in life. The Holy Spirit is always with us, and when we get off track, He gently helps make the necessary corrections; and when we fall, He is there to help pick us up and put us back in the race of our journey. We are called to stand firm, and while we are standing in a divided nation, we look around with panoramic eyes and heart to see all Christ would have us do in the midst of all the turmoil. We are to never shrink back and live in the fears the enemy would have us live. If you haven't heard by now, I would like to tell you, "we are victorious in Christ," and we have been delivered from all fears. Fear binds, but faith releases. You can live your life with faith and trust in Jesus Christ and be free, and it doesn't matter all of the negatives going on around us in many places in America.

There are so many people who come from broken or divided homes, and it becomes very difficult for them to overcome the stigma associated with the hurts they saw or were involved in. My compassion goes out to them, and having had conversations with many, it becomes very difficult for an outsider to say and do the right thing to help bring healing and restoration to the wounds. The Scripture says, "And if a house is divided against itself, that house cannot stand." There is definite proof in many homes and lives this is very true. Having seen so many of these situations in person, in most cases, the pain is evident. Many people try to cover up these pains by being active in something to keep their minds busy, or they buy and accumulate things to fill their void. May all of those affected by broken or divided homes turn to God and allow Him and His Word bring healing or fill the void.

America will never be the same again after all of the division we see and hear about today. The damage has been done to the heart of our nation, and without a strong presence of the Christian population taking right ground according to the Word of God, and praying for a spiritual awakening, things could get even worse. The Church, which is God's people, do have an appointed destiny in this world right now. We must have and demonstrate spiritual confidence in God and not in ourselves, standing up when the nation is divided, and standing firm in our convictions. We can be aggressive in our love for other people around us. It has been said each person in their lifetime has a sphere of influence of about 200 people. These would be people in our neighborhood, our workplace, and places we go every day. We can also be aggressive in our prayer life for all Americans, even those in Washington, our President, and the leaders in office, even down to state and local levels. We often have so much trouble praying for what we would call our enemies, but according to the Bible, we are to pray for them as well as our family and friends.

Allow this gentle warning to all of us: as we live in the very midst of overwhelming pressure to compromise our stand and belief in Jesus Christ, we must stand fast or be taken off of the destiny for our spiritual future. There is a battle raging, even now, for us to accept things as normal when they are not that way, and we know it. Many institutions have already caved into the demands of certain movements to stay away from lawsuits. Some church denominations have given in to areas where they know are not biblical, but in the name of keeping peace, they bow down to the demands. Churches have been divided and splintered over controversial issues because of pressure applied to the leadership. In a day of religious uncertainty, we better know what we truly believe and what the Bible says. Once we have fallen and broken our legs, it will be very difficult to ever stand firm again without the aid of crutches. Weakness sets in, and we can fall for anything at any time when pressure is applied.

In closing of this chapter, I would like to share about the "danger of neglected warnings." God, through His Word, repeatedly warns men today of the danger of sin and the need to serve Him obediently. America, God says we must repent and turn from evil. Is our nation turning its back on God, the One who has blessed us with continual blessing every day? What are you and I doing about the warnings in His Word? Would it do any good to sound the alarm or would we be ridiculed for standing up for a divided nation we love and have received so much from? I remember the story about the Titanic and how the owners said it was unsink- able. The word *Titanic* means "of exceptional strength, size, power, and being tremendous." There were 2200 people on board, and over 1500 of them died. As the Titanic pro- ceeded on the journey to America, her crew received no fewer than six messages from other ships warning of ice in the very area where she eventually struck the iceberg. This iceberg was a belt of ice 78 miles wide, directly in the path of this great ship. What was deemed unsinkable was steeped in the pride of the ability it had. It disregarded all possible danger signals.

Hebrews 3:12-15 New King James Version
(NKJV)

"Beware, brethren, lest there be in any of you
an evil heart of unbelief in departing from
the living God; but exhort one another daily,
while it is called 'Today,' lest any of you be
hardened through the deceitfulness of sin.
For we have become partakers of Christ if we
hold the beginning of our confidence steadfast to the end."

1 Peter 5:8-9 New King James Version (NKJV)

"Be sober, be vigilant; because your adver-
sary the devil walks about like a roaring lion,
seeking whom he may devour. Resist him,
steadfast in the faith, knowing that the same
sufferings are experienced by your brother-
hood in the world."

*Chapter 6*

# STAND UP & STAND STRONG, PUT ON YOUR ARMOR

As believers in Jesus Christ, we are engaged in spiritual warfare with unseen wicked forces. To overcome our enemy in the power of the Holy Spirit, we must remain determined in our confidence in God and never accept defeat.

I found this short story from the Korean War that illustrates this attitude. As enemy forces advanced, Baker Company was cut off from the rest of their unit. For several hours, no word was heard, even though headquarters repeatedly tried to communicate with the missing troops. Finally, a faint signal was received. Straining to hear, the corpsman asked, "Baker Company, do you read me?" "This is Baker Company," came the reply. "What is your situation?" asked the corpsman. "The enemy is to the east of us, the enemy is to the north of us, the enemy is to the west of us, the enemy is to the south of us." Then after a brief pause, the sergeant from Baker Company said with determination, "The enemy is not going to get away from us now" (this story was borrowed, do not know the author).

Although surrounded and outnumbered, he was thinking of victory, not defeat. Just like all of the people like you and I believe for victory in America, we do not believe just for victory, we believe from victory! Our attitudes and belief in God and His power with us, doing our part, our Commander-in-chief has already won all the victories for us. All we have to do is get up, dress up in the armor, stand up, and line up, waiting our marching orders. He will lead us to victory for our nation. Therefore, let us make ourselves available to use the tools we have been given and let us learn to stand. We just might be in the fight of our lives and the lives of the future generations of Americans. The victory belongs to everyone willing to participate with God, and the call to rally together as a people as it says in this Scripture. You probably know it by heart, but it is worthy to be used here.

2 Chronicles 7:14 New King James Version (NKJV)

"If My people who are called by My name will humble themselves, and pray and seek My face, and turn from their wicked ways, then I

will hear from heaven, and will forgive their
sin and heal their land."

1 Corinthians 15:57 New King James Version
(NKJV)

"But thanks *be* to God, who gives us the victory through our Lord Jesus Christ."

While I was on Army active duty in Germany from 1957—
1960, on many occasions, we were called to "Alert Status,"
which meant the enemy was making a move, and we had
to prepare to make a counterattack and defend our territory if the need arose. On many of those occasions, the alert
was a drill to see just how prepared we were, and to identify the changes that might need to be addressed to get us
battle ready. When you are in a large tank company, being
prepared all of the time was somewhat difficult; so much
to do in having the tank ready at all times, and then being
physically ready as a member of such a fighting force. If by
chance it was just a drill, we were graded on our status of
being prepared, and if the officers wrote us up, then came
the harsh chewing-outs and overtime work to bring the corrections needed. Being in the military really helped me in
regular life after I got out because of all of the disciplines
they taught me. It has been very valuable ever since.

Not to panic, but I believe there is a loud call going out in our nation today, and it is saying this: "Alert!"- "Alert!" – "Alert!" This is not a verbal call, but a call within to get all of us prepared for the things to come upon our USA. This call is also going out to the Church in America specifically, and I believe there are several components involved in this call. We do not want to lose you, or have you stop reading, but I have to be very honest at this point and tell the truth. Grab a rope and hang on with me as we share together.

Note: ***If America will not stand for what is right, she will fall for what is wrong.***

## 1. There Is a Call to Repentance

a. This is the ultimate call to the Church in America.
b. 2 Chronicles 7:14 New King James Version (NKJV)
"If My people who are called by My name will humble themselves, and pray and seek My face, and turn from their wicked ways, then I will hear from heaven, and will forgive their sin and heal their land."
c. Humble themselves (this seems to be very difficult for most of us, but God does so many great things in the life of a person who walks in humility).
Pray (pray without ceasing).
Seek My face.
a. Beauty of His Holiness
b. Radiance of His Glory

c. His never-ending love being shown

d. See His power and fire in His eyes

Turn from their wicked ways (read Psalms 51-David's repentant prayer)

a. He will hear from Heaven

b. He will forgive our sin

c. He will heal our land

d. As the Church and God's people, we are:

a. Called to be His people (remember this)

b. We are to love Him with all our heart, mind, and strength

c. We are to live distinctively holy lives (even when we fail, He is there)

d. Witness to our neighbors and friends (market-place outreach)

e. Disciple other Americans in the ways of the Lord

## 2. There is a Call to Rally:

a. The call to bind together as a force (not militant)

b. Come together for a common action or purpose

c. Phil 2:1-2: "If therefore if there is any consolation in Christ, if any comfort of love, if there is any fellowship of the Spirit, if any affection and compassion, 'make my joy complete by being of the same mind, maintaining the same love, united in spirit, intent on one purpose.'"

d. We are in a great spiritual battle. We have a great cause. David entered the ranks of Israel that day and said, "Is there not a cause?"

e. It's all about faith, family, and freedom. The lines of the battle are very clear. God is raising up His people to be victorious, define their enemy, and win in the name of Jesus Christ. To God be the glory.

## 3. There Is a Call to Respond (Action)

a. As free American Christian citizens we are called:

1. Help establish righteous civil government
2. To pray at all times
3. To vote (this is a great freedom we have)
4. To boldly proclaim God's Word every opportunity we have
5. To openly support and elect godly officials without fear
6. To denounce, withstand, and defeat officials who despoil our godly heritage—or defy God's eternal law by their public actions or private behavior
7. Exodus 18:21 New King James Version (NKJV)

> "Moreover you shall select from all the people able men, such as fear God, men of truth, hating covetousness; and place *such* over them *to be* rulers of thousands, rulers of hundreds, rulers of fifties, and rulers of tens."

I would like to list some of the foundations of America, and you can make your own assessment about all of these that are still intact in our nation's values.

1. Godly principles
2. Word of God (Bible)
3. Pledge of Allegiance (patriotism)
4. Respect for others
5. Honesty–in government and business practices
6. Integrity–the quality of being honest and having strong moral principles
7. Truth – not lying, but being truthful
8. Freedom–knowing "freedom is not free"
9. Moral principles
10. God's blessings
11. Right from wrong
12. Strong families and home
13. Prayer in school
14. Bible reading in school
15. Religious speech in school
16. Prayer over lunch in school
17. 10 Commandments hung on walls

We are very sure more could be added that have been taken away over the last few years, and if things do not change, we are headed to a total society that will follow the Old Testament Scripture, which says: "In those days there was no king in Israel; everyone did what was right in his own eyes" (Judges 17:6). Thousands are already doing this in America.

We will close out this chapter called: "Stand Up & Stand Strong, Put On Your Armor" with the Scripture as follows:

Ephesians 6:10-20 New King James Version (NKJV)

The Whole Armor of God

"Finally, my brethren, be strong in the Lord and in the power of His might. Put on the whole armor of God, that you may be able to stand against the wiles of the devil. For we do not wrestle against flesh and blood, but against principalities, against powers, against the rulers of the darkness of this age, against spiritual *hosts* of wickedness in the heavenly *places.* Therefore take up the whole armor of God, that you may be able to withstand in the evil day, and having done all, to stand.

Stand therefore, having girded your waist with truth, having put on the breastplate of righteousness, and having shod your feet with the preparation of the gospel of peace; above all, taking the shield of faith with which you will be able to quench all the fiery darts of the wicked one. And take the helmet of salvation, and the sword of the Spirit, which

47

is the word of God; praying always with all prayer and supplication in the Spirit, being watchful to this end with all perseverance and supplication for all the saints— and for me, that utterance may be given to me, that I may open my mouth boldly to make known the mystery of the gospel, for which I am an ambassador in chains; that in it I may speak boldly, as I ought to speak."

Daily, we get up and get dressed for the day. We may lay out exactly what we are going to wear to work or whatever the occasion. Some people put on their weekly best, and on Sunday, if you are going to church, we like to look good so others can see us in case we have something new to display. There is nothing wrong with looking great because it makes us feel good about ourselves.

We need to talk about the Scripture above as we fight for America today and for the great future it needs to have. Since we're fighting against enemies in the spirit world, we are going to need some God-supplied special equipment not only for the defense but also for the offense. Since this is talking about us putting on the whole armor of God, this means we must put on all He has provided and not leave any of it off. Each piece of armor has a distinct reason for its use for our protection. The enemy is always looking for an area that is not guarded, and this will be his area of attack on us spiritually; when we are hit in a specific area, it could also cause physical issues eventually.

Sometimes when we are attacked by an individual for no reason we can think of, we should respond by praying for the person and not attack their person, but the spirit who may have caused them to act the way they are. When you have the armor on, the fiery darts do not have the ability to do you harm, and you become victorious over the situation. Most of the time, it sounds like it is easier said than doing the battle the right way.

The information we are sharing is for you personally, so you can be involved in the solutions for America on the basis God calls you to do. Each of us should be ready at any time to man our battle stations, whether it be on your knees praying, writing letters to senators, congressmen, or the President himself; making telephone calls to voice your concerns, and letting leadership know your voice needs to be heard. We all need and have to do something because as we bind together in the realm of the physical and the spiritual, we can become a force for change in America. Will you become involved and do your part and use your God-given calling for a supernatural change in our nation?

Romans 12:1-2 New King James Version (NKJV)

Living Sacrifices to God

"I beseech you therefore, brethren, by the mercies of God, that you present your bodies a living sacrifice, holy, acceptable to God, *which is* your reasonable service. And do not be conformed to this world, but be transformed by the renewing of your mind, that you may prove what *is* that good and acceptable and perfect will of God."

PRAYER: Prayer is the energy that we take with us into each battle. If you haven't figured out, we can't fight against the enemy in our own strength. "Praying always" does not mean we are always saying a prayer to God. It means we are always staying in communion with God. That way, we are ready for any surprises the enemy would attack us with. Do not just have your focus on yourself and your needs, but be in prayer for others, and this attitude can bring victory in your life! Stand up and stand strong for America and yourself.

*Chapter 7*

# STAND UP & STAND FIRM

W hen I was serving in the U.S. Army in Germany, there were many times guard duty came up, and the requirements for this duty were very stringent (strict, precise, and exacting). On one occasion, I was on guard duty and being taken several miles from camp, the place was near the woods in a very lonely place, and I was not familiar with the territory. I was told to stand guard there and protect a nearby road and observe any activity that could be going on as far as I could see. I was to relieve another soldier, and of course I knew to stand firm in this place for the normal 4-6 hours before a replacement would come. To this day, one of the 11 General Orders that we had to memorize, I can still remember. The order is this: "To be especially watchful at night, and during the time for challenging, to challenge all persons on or near my post, and to allow no one to pass without proper authority." We were given the password to challenge any intruders that might come along, and if they did not know the password, they could be the enemy.

Guard duty was always very lonely, and you were not to talk to anyone, even if they were available, as you were to be constantly on the alert for suspicious activity. They didn't leave a way of communication, so I was dependent on them coming back in the allotted time and then I could give the report of any activity. I stood there for 4 hours, then six hours, and time went on and on. Luckily, I brought some C-Rations and water to sustain my hunger and thirst. Nightfall came, and still the replacement did not come. My replacement did not come the first night, the next day, or the following night. They had forgotten and left me out there alone for over 30 hours, as I can remember. They finally remembered because I was missing the formations back at the base, and they did not understand where I was. By the time they got to me, there was a heaping bunch of anger built up inside of me, to say it lightly; I was mad, but in the Army, there is not much you can do about a situation like that.

The duty officer himself came out with my replacement, and they started apologizing profusely, and I stood my ground in anger. Well, to make a long story short, because of the error, I was given a three-day pass and could do whatever I wanted to do. I got over my anger, but it was hard to forget. I played it up to get the maximum benefit I could from the situation. When out there by myself, I never left my post, and

I stood firm in my duty, because from memory the General Orders for guard duty were engrained in my mind, and I knew I was to never leave my post without being properly relieved by another soldier who was on duty, or I could be court-martialed, and I did not need that on my record.

This story was shared to be a reminder that we as Christians have an assigned place to be involved in the army of God. When we receive Jesus Christ into our hearts and lives, we are given specific gifts to be utilized for the expansion of the kingdom of God. Each one of us is very important to Him, and every gift is empowered by the Holy Spirit for us to carry it out as we grow in the Lord through His Word. America truly needs the power of your gift to be in operation, to bring our nation back to where it should be. The Lord wants to bless as you become responsible to help touch your family, friends, and neighbors, which in turn will bring change to America. Stand up, stand firm, and do not vacate your assigned post of love for the Lord and for America.

I would like to share with you about three young men in the Bible who understood how to stand up and stand firm in a situation that was very tough and trying in their lives.

Daniel 3:19-26 New King James Version (NKJV)

Saved in Fiery Trial

"Then Nebuchadnezzar was full of fury, and the expression on his face changed toward Shadrach, Meshach, and Abed-Nego. He spoke and commanded that they heat the furnace seven times more than it was usually heated. And he commanded certain mighty men of valor who were in his army to bind Shadrach, Meshach, and Abed-Nego, and cast them into the burning fiery furnace. Then these men were bound in their coats, their trousers, their turbans, and their other garments, and were cast into the midst of the burning fiery furnace. Therefore, because the king's command was urgent, and the furnace exceedingly hot, the flame of the fire killed those men who took up Shadrach, Meshach, and Abed-Nego. And these three men, Shadrach, Meshach, and Abed-Nego, fell down bound into the midst of the burning fiery furnace. Then King Nebuchadnezzar was astonished; and he rose in haste and spoke, saying to his counselors, 'Did we not cast three men bound into the midst of the fire?'

They answered and said to the king, 'True, O king.'

'Look!' he answered, 'I see four men loose, walking in the midst of the fire; and they are not hurt, and the form of the fourth is like the Son of God.' Then Nebuchadnezzar went near the mouth of the burning fiery furnace and spoke, saying, 'Shadrach, Meshach, and Abed-Nego, servants of the Most High God, come out, and come here.' Then Shadrach, Meshach, and Abed-Nego came from the midst of the fire."

The three Hebrew young men were charged with not bowing down to an idol. They were also challenged with a question, "Who is the God who shall deliver you out of my hands?" (Daniel 3:15). They were threatened to be thrown in the fiery furnace. They thought about it and answered, "If that is the case, our God whom we serve is able to deliver us from the burning fiery furnace, and He will deliver us from your hand, O king. But if not, let it be known to you, O king, that we do not serve your gods, nor will we worship the gold image which you have set up" (Daniel 3:17, 18). They were saying to the king, "You will receive no compromise from us!"

After I placed the Scripture in the storyline, it became so real life to me; and after reading it three times, I thought how so many people in America have begun bowing down to idols and they do not even realize it. They are not literally bowing down, but the things of this world have crowded out the spiritual life they used to live. I am not being judgmental because I have probably done the same thing at times. Many people in our nation and around the world have a distorted view of who God is, based on bad information coming from bad sources. We become what we watch and what we listen to. It is so easy to fill our mind and hearts with junk. Garbage in, garbage out. The truth is becoming so distorted, and people are going to accept what they hear as truth if there is something in it for them. We all have to guard our minds because this is the enemy's place to get us to act on his information, and then it goes to our hearts and we began to live a lie and do not even know it. Paul warned us in the Bible the times are going to become perilous, difficult, and desperate.

2 Timothy 3:1-5 New King James Version (NKJV)

Perilous Times and Perilous Men

"But know this, that in the last days perilous times will come: For men will be lovers of themselves, lovers of money, boasters, proud, blasphemers, disobedient to parents, unthankful, unholy, unloving, unforgiving, slanderers, without self-control, brutal, despisers of good, traitors, headstrong, haughty, lovers of pleasure rather than lovers of God, having a form of godliness but denying its power. And from such people turn away!"

Have these times arrived in America? The times he was talking about will have the following conclusions: it will be harder to walk with God because so many other things are being dangled before us to cause distraction. It will be much harder to keep marriages together and strong. Just look around and you can find this to be true in our society. It will be far more difficult, and it will be threatening for Christian men and women to stand for the godly things in the business world and society. Whether we would like to admit it or not, the activity of the enemy will be hard to handle, and more powerful. We know he is a defeated foe because Jesus took authority over him, and we can be winners in our lives in the name of Jesus Christ. There are other things, like an increase in crime, immorality, temptation, and heresy will become more rampant. So many more things are going on, but we will not single them out, not out of fear, but because this book is destined to get Americans to wake up, stand up, and look up. We will cover all of these before we get through. Let me ask you this question, what are we to do or what are you to do?

2 Timothy 4:1-5 New King James Version (NKJV)

Preach the Word

"I charge you therefore before God and the Lord Jesus Christ, who will judge the living and the dead at His appearing and His kingdom: Preach the word! Be ready in season and out of season. Convince, rebuke, exhort, with all longsuffering and teaching. For the time will come when they will not endure sound doctrine, but according to their own desires, because they have itching ears, they will heap up for themselves teachers; and they will turn their ears away from the truth, and be turned aside to fables. But you be watchful in all things, endure afflictions, do the work of an evangelist, fulfill your ministry."

You might say, after reading the Scripture above, I am not an evangelist like Timothy. If you are a born-again Christian, you can share your testimony and love others into the kingdom of God. You do not have to know the entire Bible to love others, have prayer with them, spend time, or have a meal to "love the family into fellowship with God." In love and compassion, share the Gospel introduction to a life with Christ. We must have enough of the love of Christ to help snatch people out of the hands of the enemy, Satan.

As this Scripture says, there are three things we can do: make the Scripture our standard. "Preach the Word." Be ready in season and out of season, and have your spiritual antenna up as high as it will go, so you can hear the Holy Spirit guiding and instructing you. Lastly, take a stand and say to yourself: "I will do what is right, whether anybody else is doing it or not." The world around us needs thousands of Americans with a heart after God to take a stand, and He will use you to help change other hearts, and in the process, you will have a heart change to believe you can do all things through Christ who will strengthen you to do all He has called you to do. Stand up and stand firm.

*Chapter 8*

# STAND UP WHEN IT SEEMS NO ONE ELSE WILL

hen I knew this book was supposed to be written, and sensing a mandate to accomplish the task, I had a lot of questions that were going over in my mind. I didn't challenge the Lord about it, so I just accepted it by faith in Him to get it done for His glory. My wife Tillie and I have walked by faith for over 40 years, and God has been very faithful in every season of our lives on this journey. We have learned to trust and obey, for there seemed to be no other way for us to accomplish the missions He had for us. We are older and hopefully wiser, and can help others reach their destiny in Christ as long as we live. Almost daily, there are opportunities to show His love and compassion to someone in the marketplace or where our feet take us in our walk with Him.

As this chapter came to my mind, as with the previous chapters, I knew it would be a task for me to do this without the Holy Spirit giving me the directions to reach out to hurting people as well as a hurting nation. I prayed about this and I know you are the very important person we will go forward to share His love with. We have written some very challenging things for some of you to try and understand and find out exactly what you are supposed to do for America. Some of you do not comprehend some of the Scriptures and spiritual directions we would like to see happen in the future for everyone in this nation. There was a quickening in my heart about people in America who might read this book, and you do not know Jesus Christ as your Savior and Lord, or you might have strayed away from Him. The things of this world have taken their toll on your life and you might be in a mess yourself. We want to help take you from the mess and share the message of hope and restoration with you right now.

We will call this: "This Is Your Life or Is This Your Life?" The call is for all Christians and Americans to be able to stand up in Christ, and the power of the Holy Spirit to do exploits to expand your life and to maximize your abilities and bring His joy to your life. The Scripture we will share with you now should help in determining where you are in life now. Receiving Jesus Christ into your heart is only the beginning of the Christian life as there is so much more to live for in the freedom He has for you.

Matthew 6:25-34 New King James Version (NKJV)

Do Not Worry

"Therefore I say to you, do not worry about your life, what you will eat or what you will drink; nor about your body, what you will put on. Is not life more than food and the body more than clothing? Look at the birds of the air, for they neither sow nor reap nor gather into barns; yet your heavenly Father feeds them. Are you not of more value than they? Which of you by worrying can add one cubit to his stature?"

"So why do you worry about clothing? Consider the lilies of the field, how they grow: they neither toil nor spin; and yet I say to you that even Solomon in all his glory was not arrayed like one of these. Now if God so clothes the grass of the field, which today is, and tomorrow is thrown into the oven, will He not much more clothe you, O you of little faith?"

"Therefore do not worry, saying, 'What shall we eat?' or 'What shall we drink?' or 'What shall we wear?' For after all these things the Gentiles seek. For your heavenly Father knows that you need all these things. But seek first the kingdom of God and His righteousness, and all these things shall be added to you. Therefore do not worry about tomorrow, for tomorrow will worry about its own things. Sufficient for the day is its own trouble."

1. This is your life, by loving the Lord your God.

   a. And you shall love the Lord Your God with all your heart and with all your soul and with all your strength. (Deuteronomy 6:5)

2. This is your life, by obeying His voice.

   a. My sheep hear My voice, and I know them, and they follow me. (John 10:27)

3. This is your life, by holding fast to Him.

   a. You shall fear the Lord your God; you shall serve Him and to Him you shall hold fast, and take oaths in His name. (Deuteronomy 10:20)

1 John 5:11-13 New King James Version (NKJV)

"And this is the testimony: that God has given us eternal life, and this life is in His Son. He who has the Son has life; he who does not have the Son of God does not have life. These things I have written to you who believe in the name of the Son of God, that you may know that you have eternal life, and that you may continue to believe in the name of the Son of God."

When you invite and receive the Lord Jesus into your life, He actually and literally comes to live in you by the Holy Spirit of God. Living the Christian life does not mean trying to live like Christ, it means trusting Christ to live in you and through you; Christ in you, the hope of glory. If you think of Christ simply being near you rather than living in you, your constant effort will be to get closer to Him or to get Him closer to you. This will result in frustration, discouragement, and defeat.

Paul said it so plainly for us to know and receive in the following Scripture:

Galatians 2:20 New King James Version (NKJV)

> " I have been crucified with Christ; it is no
> longer I who live, but Christ lives in me; and
> the life which I now live in the flesh I live by
> faith in the Son of God, who loved me and
> gave Himself for me."

Know this, believe this, and the Christian life will become real and exciting for you! You might be asking right now, "How can I get Jesus to come into my life?" Read this Scripture.

Revelation 3:20 New King James Version (NKJV)

> " Behold, I stand at the door and knock. If
> anyone hears My voice and opens the door,
> I will come in to him and dine with him, and
> he with Me."

Jesus is telling you today the door to your heart opens from the inside so you by your own must open the door by faith in Him, and ask Him to come in and forgive your sins (repentance) and give you eternal life. He will come in and be your Savior and Lord as you receive and accept Him, and He will give you a new life forever. Now you can stand up and declare to the world you are a new person and old things have passed away and behold all things become new.

Your new nature will take you on a different and exciting life's journey, and the Holy Spirit living in you will be your guide, and lead you into paths of righteousness.

You have been set free by Jesus Christ. Jesus gained absolute victory and total freedom for you when He was raised from the dead. The moment you received Jesus into your heart and life, this victory and freedom became yours. It is the knowledge of the truth that enables you to walk and live in freedom. The Bible, the Word of God, now becomes your road map to keep you walking on the straight path of life you desire. Glory to God you are free. You are free from the powers of Satan. Not only are you free from the powers of darkness, but you are also freed into the kingdom of light. You are free to love, you are free to help others, you are free to enjoy the abundant life, and you are free to do acts of righteousness. Jesus Christ has made you absolutely free in every area of your life as you trust and follow Him.

Hebrews 11:6 New King James Version (NKJV)

"But without faith *it is* impossible to please *Him,* for he who comes to God must believe that He is, and *that* He is a rewarder of those who diligently seek Him."

Now we will turn our thoughts to getting directions to be able to "rest in the Lord." This is very possible, and as

Christians, we need to take time to rest and enjoy His presence. We all look for times of refreshing in knowing Christ and enjoying our relationship daily with Him in the spiritual realm. Whether we are just sitting in our chair at home reading the Bible, walking around a trail at the lake listening to Gospel music, or just being alone with Him in a quiet place special to you and Him only. This time is very necessary as we prepare our heart, mind, and body for the battles that blindside us on occasion. Now in America, we are in a spiritual battle for the soul of our nation, and we have to be very prepared to help tear down the strongholds that bind our future in God. Psalm ll:3 says: "If the foundations are destroyed, What can the righteous do?" Great question isn't it? Ponder your thoughts on that Scripture for your quiet time today. For you, today, read the Scripture below, and we will discuss it in detail.

Psalm 37:1-7 New King James Version (NKJV)

The Heritage of the Righteous and the Calamity of the Wicked

A Psalm *of David.*

**37** Do not fret because of evildoers,
Nor be envious of the workers of iniquity.
² For they shall soon be cut down like the grass,
And wither as the green herb.

³ Trust in the Lord, and do good;
Dwell in the land, and feed on His faithfulness.
⁴ Delight yourself also in the Lord,
And He shall give you the desires of your heart.
⁵ Commit your way to the Lord,
Trust also in Him,
And He shall bring *it* to pass.
⁶ He shall bring forth your righteousness as
the light,
And your justice as the noonday.
⁷ Rest in the Lord, and wait patiently for Him;
Do not fret because of him who prospers
in his way,
Because of the man who brings wicked
schemes to pass.

Now picture in your mind a ladder, and you are going to the top using six steps, and each one has a significant meaning in your journey to find "rest in the Lord." Let's build our ladder together (this way up).

Step 1. **DO NOT FRET**. Vs.1 (fretfulness and envy are sins that are their own punishments; they are the uneasiness of the spirit and the rottenness of the bones. We help ourselves by not being fretful.)

Step 2. **TRUST IN THE LORD.** Vs.3 (Trust in Him: His favor, His providence, His promises, His grace; and have a diligence to serve Him.)

Step 3. **DELIGHT YOURSELF IN THE LORD.** Vs.4 (We must delight ourselves in who He is, in His beauty, His goodness, His bountiful love, His kindness, and graciousness. He has not promised to gratify all of our appetites. What is the desire of the heart of a committed follower of Christ? It is this, to know, love, and live to God; to please Him and to be pleased in Him.)

Step 4. **COMMIT YOUR WAY TO THE LORD.** Vs.5 (We must roll it off ourselves so as not to afflict and perplex ourselves with thoughts about future events.) The question we can ask ourselves is, "Why pray when we can worry?" So we need to refer it to God, leave it to Him, so He can dispose of all our concerns as He pleases.

Step 5. "**REST IN THE LORD, and wait patiently for Him;** Vs.7 (Be well satisfied that He will make all things work for good for us, though we know not how or which way!)

Step 6. "**REST**" (to put trust in to place or hold in support; to have foundation; to lean on.) After you have taken these steps of faith in the Lord, you will gain rest in Him, and you are prepared to get to know Him better and you can have great fellowship, and be prepared to become a great warrior for His purposes, your future, and the future of America.

Stand up for Jesus Christ and America when it seems no one else you know will!

# Section Three

*It's Time to Wake Up, Stand Up, Look Up*

# LOOK UP

**Put on Christ**

Luke 21:28 New King James Version (NKJV)

"Now when these things begin to happen, look up and lift up your heads, because your redemption draws near."

# Introduction Into Section Three

Jim Jamieson

Everyone has a story to tell. I found this out after listening to many people over the years that took time to share their hearts with me. Some of the stories were tough to listen to because of the pain and suffering people were going through. The answers to help in most of their stories were hard to come by from me, but the Holy Spirit would come, and the tears would flow, and healing would come in many instances. The Holy Spirit can do what we can't if we just let Him. He will come when we invite Him, and we recognize our weaknesses, then He does a miracle in someone's life right before our eyes. Prayer is very powerful when our trust is in His ability and not ours. We do our part to love and listen, and He liberates the issues in their lives. This is a great time to share the following Scripture:

John 14:25-27 New King James Version (NKJV)

"These things I have spoken to you while being present with you. But the Helper, the Holy Spirit, whom the Father will send in My name, He will teach you all things, and bring to your remembrance all things that I said to you. Peace I leave with you, My peace I give to you; not as the world gives do I give to you. Let not your heart be troubled, neither let it be afraid."

The title of this section of the book is "Look Up," and with the help of the Holy Spirit, we can be constantly looking up for the return of Jesus Christ. There are so many prophecies and Scriptures that give us the indication the time is drawing very near. Many have been fulfilled and now the Gospel message is being declared almost around the world, and I believe we will see the hearts of men, women, and children turning to the Lord and declaring their faith in Him, instead of having their faith in mankind. Many will be falling away from their faith because of the cares of this world, situations, anger about specific things in their lives, and losing hope for their future. Many already have gone away from the Lord. They developed a distorted view of Him because they have not seen Him work in their lives the way they wanted Him to. We need to pray for all of those who are seeking for direction in their lives. May there be a real move to draw people back to a relationship with Jesus Christ because He loves everyone. "A change of heart and mind will lead to a change of direction."

Allow me to ask you a few questions that could cause you to look up to Jesus Christ, and let Him bring total confirmation to your heart for your eternal future. This is important!

1. Are you a lonely person? You are this way no matter how many friends you have, and when you are alone, you are miserable in your heart, and you cry yourself to sleep at night wondering what is wrong.

2. Are you a defeated person? You feel defeated because no matter how hard you try in life to be popular or recognized, in your mind, you always fall short of your own expectations when you see others excel and have what you couldn't achieve.

3. Are you troubled in your heart? Do you constantly look back to your past and bring up the negative things about who you are? You look in the mirror and do not like what you see because of past failures; is this you? Living in guilt and condemnation heaped upon yourself, and others see you in a different way completely, and you do not believe them. You have formed your own opinion and your life is full of gloom, despair, and agony on me. Look up to Jesus Christ, read the Bible, and find out what He says about you.

4. Are you an insecure person? Are you fearful most of the time, what others might be saying about you? Do you let other people's opinions control your life now and the future God has for you? This reminds me of the story of a person who was so insecure that he didn't like to go to football games because every time the team huddled up, he thought they were talking about him. Now that is insecure. This is a condition that may be unpleasant and not peaceful. Trust in the Lord and do not lean to your own understanding, but always acknowledge Him, and He will direct your path in life. Victory is yours today!

The following four chapters under the title of "Look Up" are written by four great American ladies, who will share with you from their hearts about situations they were blind-sided with and were not expecting. Each story is and can be heart and life-changing for those who read and apply the love and wisdom with which they share. If you relate to any of their stories, may God touch your heart and life, and bring peace to you in a supernatural way.

God bless today and forever is our prayer for you.

*Chapter 9*

# PEACE IN A SEVERE STORM

### By Tillie Jamieson

My name is Priscilla "Tillie" Green Jamieson, and I grew up in the wonderful town of Wheeler in the Texas Panhandle. My love for doing hair and visiting with people has developed into fifty-nine years of being a beautician. I am the mother of Tina, Todd, Rodney, and Tiffany Jamieson, and wife of an amazing man, Jim Jamieson, for almost fifty-nine years. My love for the Lord is full of gratitude for Him guiding my life.

When you are young parents, never in your wildest dreams, do you think you will lose a child. But that's what happened to us. We had four delightful children in four and one-half years, named Tina, Todd, Rodney, and Tiffany. Life was demanding, to say the least, and in fact, I went back to work to rest!

It seems like in families there is usually one child more prone to accidents or things happening to them. That's how it seemed to be with our third child, Rodney. One day when he was small, he came in from outdoors and said a turtle bit the end of his toe off, and sure enough, when I looked, there was a chunk gone. Then one day, the kids were in the backyard playing, and I did not know about it, but they had found an old, rusted, jagged screwdriver and were throwing it up in the air playing a game called "chicken," it came down and hit Rod (we called him Rod) in the head, requiring a trip to the emergency room for stitches. You will find as my story goes along, we almost had a pass to the emergency room every month or so. There was a cartoon in the newspaper called "Family Circus," and some of my friends thought I might be sending in stories from our family. Most of this happened when our kids were all under eight years old.

We got so busy, and were tired, so we did not find time to go to church. However, when Tina started kindergarten at the Lutheran Church, she came home and said we needed to go to church so she could get a star on her chart at school. So we did; at least, I took Tina and Tiffany some, so Tina could get a star.

Life sometimes gets to be a blur. I was working doing hair, and Jimmy was working hard to make a living. The kids were active, lively children. I remember one time while the kids were across the street at the babysitters, Todd and another boy staying there, turned a bicycle upside down and were spinning the wheel with a card attached to the wheel with a clothespin to make that certain sound like a little motor. Well, Todd got his finger caught in the chain, and it cut the end of his finger off. We were able to get to the emergency room and have it sewn back on. I'm sure this is reminding you of some incidents that happened in your life, too. Come to think of it, Todd seemed to have his share of accidents, as you will see as my story goes along.

When the kids were small, before car seats were required and before cars had child safety locks, we were driving home and I had to make a left turn on the highway. The kids were all in the backseat, and Rod popped the door handle open and fell out on the highway. He was about three and one-half years old. Luckily, I was going slow enough he wasn't hurt, except for some scratches, and no traffic was coming. He was tough.

It was soon after that, on Mother's Day, Jimmy decided to play in a golf tournament in Perryton, Texas. I was mad about that, so I loaded the kids in the car and found some material to tie the doors of the car so the kids couldn't open them, and went over 2 hours to Wheeler, Texas, my home-town. Tiffany was about a year old. I stopped at the local Dairy Cream to get ice cream cones. I got out of the car to go to the window to order, carrying Tiffany. The car was parked on a slight incline, and when I got out, one of the kids pulled the car out of park gear, and it started rolling towards a cinderblock building down the way. When I turned to see what was happening, I quickly threw Tiffany down in the dirt, and started running as hard as I could to jump in the car and stop before it hit the building. Thankfully, I was able to and then went back to pick Tiffany up out of the dirt and stop her crying. I honestly do not remember if we got ice cream cones, but I do remember the stares I got from the people watching what had just happened. Tiffany wasn't hurt, only some scratches. It seems Tiffany was the only one of our kids that didn't have stitches at the emergency room, only a butterfly Band-Aid when she stuck her finger in the snow cone machine at the swimming pool.

I could tell you any number of stories that we went through with the kids, like when Todd was about seven years old and he did a flip off the side of the city swimming pool, and busted the top of his head, and again to the emergency room to have him sewn up. Or the time Tina was riding her new ten-speed bicycle down the hill on Canyon Street where we lived, and she nearly cut her Achilles tendon on the sharp bicycle pedal. Again, we went to the emergency room for stitches. You may be beginning to wonder if we ever had any good times with the kids. Yes, we did! However, have you noticed that the negative ones always stay in your mind more vividly?

Now, this gets to the incident that started the change in our lives. Once again, I had all of the kids in the car as I was driving, and from the backseat, Rod said, "I swallowed a nail." I said "What?" while still driving, and he said again, "I swallowed a nail." He wasn't coughing or anything to alarm me, and we were nearly home, so I drove on home. He was about four years old, and where he would have gotten a nail in the backseat only heaven knows. I told you at the start of this story we had active children. Well, when we got home, Rod didn't complain, and I just dismissed it. However, a few days later, the babysitter asked me if I knew Rod's bowel movements were black. He still used a child's potty chair. She asked if I knew what that meant, and I didn't, and she said it could mean internal bleeding. Then, that made me remember about him saying he had swallowed a nail. That began our trips to the doctor, and X-rays that very distinctly showed a one and one-half inch metal screw lodged in his intestine. We X-rayed every day for a week to see if it moved, or we would need to do surgery to dislodge it; meanwhile, watching his bowel movements to see if it came through. Amazingly one day, it didn't show up on the X-ray, nor did we find it in the stool. Whew! We thought that was over! But sometime after that, Rod began complaining of his "butt" hurting, and he began having trouble walking. It was summertime, and I thought he might have fallen at the swimming pool as kids loved going to the city pool and usually "ran" instead of walking around it.

I had hurt my back and was having some trouble walking, so when Rod would cry out in the night, I'd crawl to his bedroom, and then we would crawl to the bathroom. That's when we went to the doctor and got the diagnosis that he had leukemia (his spleen was enlarged). He was about four and one-half years old. That was in 1970. Later, I read that too much exposure to radiation on a small body mass could cause leukemia. Now that's not from the doctor, but after the Chernobyl nuclear plant blew up in Russia, and other articles I read, lead me to believe we may have X-rayed him too much. Medically, that may not have been the cause.

Rod was hospitalized for a month in Amarillo, Texas, so began our ordeal with Rod and leukemia. Then we started on a chemotherapy regimen every three weeks. The bone marrow tests were horrible; Rod screaming at the top of his lungs as they pushed the huge needle through his hip flesh into his hip bone. I could hardly stand it for him.

Rod was able to start kindergarten and was able to go seven months. The doctor told us to guard him from chickenpox; for some reason, chickenpox had a severe adverse effect on leukemia. But an outbreak happened at school, and Rod got the chickenpox. You've never seen a child with so many poxes on him. The doctor immediately took him off all of his chemo medicine, and we waited to see what would happen.

In the meantime, of the 19 months and three hospital stays in the Amarillo hospital, Jimmy's boss in Guymon, Martin Ramirez, who was a wonderful Christian, asked a young pastor in town, Ed Modrick, to come to the hospital to visit us. He did on many occasions, and that love and concern began the process of changing our lives. The stress of Rod's illness and life itself had deteriorated Jimmy and my marriage. In fact, just before Rod got sick, we were on the brink of divorce.

So Ed Modrick came to the hospital, and if Rod said he wanted a lariat rope, the next trip, Ed brought it. For some reason, Rod liked cowboy stuff. For Christmas, he asked for black cowboy boots and a black cowboy hat (but he liked the Washington Redskins football team, figure that out!) When we'd be back home in Guymon, Ed would come get all the kids and take them out to Delia Tomlinson's farm to ride the horse. Ed had begun loving us into the kingdom of God.

Rod got very ill in March 1972, the chickenpox had weakened him, and then he got bi-lateral pneumonia, and we rushed back to the hospital in Amarillo. That stay was just before Easter. Jimmy had been there with us until Thursday, and we decided he'd go home and get the kids and bring them to Amarillo to see Rod. On Friday morning, Rod took a turn for the worse, and I called our good friends, Dick and Frankie Jackson, who had a plane, to see if they could get Jimmy back as soon as possible. They tried, but Jimmy didn't make it before Rod died. That was Good Friday before Easter; not so good to me.

That night after we got back to Guymon, the pastor where I'd gone to church, and Ed Modrick, came to our house to see us. Rod had said some curse words that morning, and I didn't know anything about salvation, so I thought God might not let him into heaven. Ed said no, he was under the age of accountability (Rod was 6 now) and was repeating what he had heard others say. In a loving way, Ed said the people Rod had learned those words from needed to clean up their mouths. In my heart, I was saying I'd never cuss again, and unknown to me, Jimmy was making some life changes too. That night, I had a dream as real as if it were really happening. I dreamed Rod was on an escalator going up into the clouds, waving a palm branch as happy as he could be. When he was happy, he was smiling as big as he could! I know the Lord gave me that dream, or vision, or whatever it was, to assure me Rod went to heaven.

Rod's funeral was the day after Easter, 1972. Two weeks after he died, we went to the church Ed Modrick pastored, and we went forward at the altar call and accepted and received the Lord Jesus Christ into our hearts and home. Our lives have never been the same since then. It was like Jimmy had a Damascus Road experience; he quit drinking, quit cussing, quit smoking, and quit playing golf so much. We got involved in the Apostolic Faith Church that Ed pastored. Jimmy became the spiritual leader of our household. He, later on, became a preacher and a pastor, eventually, and an evangelist doing patriotic rallies across the U.S. and traveled to other countries, spreading the Gospel message of the life-changing power of Jesus Christ. We truly say Ed showed us the love of Jesus and loved us into the kingdom of God. As a result, the Lord has taken us on a journey of purpose and direction only the Lord could have orchestrated and brought about.

Even as the years have gone by, I still want to thank all of our wonderful friends and family that helped us while Rod was sick; my wonderful customers and co-workers at the beauty shop who span over fifty years; the people of Guymon, Oklahoma, that started a fund for us as we had just let our health insurance lapse, for financial reasons, just before Rod got sick. The fund paid for Rod's hospitalization and his funeral. There's no way this side of heaven to know all the people that prayed for us through all this, and we're eternally grateful.

I'm glad Tina, Todd, Tiffany, and Jimmy have given me grace when I probably didn't handle some of the situations as I should have.

As a result of Rod's death, our lives changed, and all of our family knows the Lord. I've said sometimes it takes someone a lifetime to accomplish their purpose on earth; perhaps Rod accomplished his in 6 years.

Family, thank you.

I'm so grateful for our children and their mates, grand-children, and great grandchildren. Thank you, Lord, for Tina, Landry, Fallon, and our precious great-grandchildren, Everett, Archer, & Bennett. For our grandson, Jamieson, each is a blessing. Also, for Todd and Jody and our grand-daughters Rachel & Aubrie, a unique blessing in each one. Then, Tiffany and Jason and our grandson, Cameron, who is the oldest grandchild. My heart is so full of gratitude for each part of our family, and the special blessings and the thoughts each one brings to my heart and mind. Thank you, Jimmy, and your godly leadership and wisdom for our family. Thank you, Lord, and thank you all of my family! I love you!

Thank you to all of our extended families and our dear friends who demonstrated the very unconditional love of God during the time we needed your support. We still remember all of the kindness you showed. God bless you all. Thank you!

I also want to thank the Lord for the peace He's brought in my life. I love the Scripture and I want to pass it on to you. "Now may the Lord of peace Himself give you peace always in every way. The Lord be with you all" (2 Thessalonians 3:16 NKJ).

# Chapter 10

## FAITH ABOVE MY FAILURE

### By Tina Link

My name is Tina Link, and I am the daughter of Jim and Tillie Jamieson. I have lived in the Dallas, TX area since 1983, where I attended Fountain Gate Bible College and earned a degree in Christian education.

After working in education for 25 years, I made a career change in 2014 to city government. I love my job and the people with whom I work.

I am blessed to be the mom of two wonderful sons, Landry and Jamieson. Landry and his beautiful wife, Fallon, made me a "Lolli" with three amazing grandsons.

2020 will bring more family blessings as Jamieson and his fiancée Hannah will be getting married. I am so thrilled at gaining another precious daughter-in-love.

I love the verses in Isaiah 43:18-19, "Forget the former things; do not dwell on the past. See, I am doing a new thing! Now it springs up; do you not perceive it? I am making a way in the wilderness and streams in the wasteland." God is ready to reveal new and precious promises to us as we focus on Him and not our past.

Remember being young and all the dreams about what you would be when you grew up? My dream was to be Miss America, a teacher, a wife, and a mom. I mean, for a little girl born in the 60s, those were the ultimate! Unfortunately, the Miss America thing did not work out, but the others did... and didn't.

Being the oldest of four children raised in a small town was filled with highs and lows. Since my parents were blessed with four beautiful children in the span of four and a half years, life was mostly chaotic. I was the oldest, so I had more responsibility at an early age. It was a simple but fun life with family and friends living close by. It was true community.

I realized that more than ever, when in 1972, my youngest brother Rodney passed away. At only six years old, he had been battling leukemia for two years. I was only eight years old, but it was a time I will never forget. I remember how my dad came to tell my brother, my sister, and me that Rodney was in heaven with Jesus, and then he hugged and comforted us. Not long after that, my aunt came and told us that we needed to "be good and not cry" when we saw our mom because she was going through a very difficult time. I can still see my mom sitting in that kitchen chair when I saw her for the first time after Rodney's death. She looked so tired, and all I remember doing was going up to her with tears, saying, "I'm so sorry Rodney died!" She hugged me and held me. It's a moment I will never forget. During that time, we were surrounded by family and friends, and I never really felt alone.

Through that tragedy, we had a transformation in our family. My parents became Christians because of the love of a local pastor to our family throughout my brother's sickness. It truly was the turning point in the destiny of our family.

At an early age, we discovered that I could sing, and that became my go-to talent. I was singing in church, traveling and singing, singing for weddings, getting to play the part of Maria in our high school musical; it was what I did and what I loved. Then there was that audition for a music scholarship to a college (which shall remain nameless, with a song I never should have sung), and the letter of rejection telling me that music might not be the field I should pursue...gulp.

What! I mean music was my life! Little did I know that this would be a beginning life lesson in how MY plan for my life might not be THE plan for my life.

I became a Christian at 10 years old and always had a belief in God, Jesus, and the Holy Spirit, and I knew that I was going to go to heaven when I died. Nothing was going to change my mind about that, so I ultimately decided I wanted to go to a Bible college. Not just any Bible college, but one that was 500 MILES AWAY FROM HOME! Yikes! Not only was I moving away from everything that I had known and loved, I was going where I knew absolutely no one! I will never ever forget the first time I had to merge onto Highway 75 in Dallas. OH, MY GOODNESS!! I have lived in a town of 6,000 people where everyone knew everyone, and now I am about to die at 19 years old on a Dallas highway! Well, that is a tad dramatic, but that is how I felt. All of a sudden, the adventure of being on my own, away from everyone I knew and loved, became very real. Thankfully, it did not take long to make lifelong friends.

We were always teased that most girls came to Bible college to get their "MRS." degree, which was mostly true, even though we hated admitting it. Because I had not dated much in high school, I genuinely felt that I was going to meet Mr. Right, and he was going to love Jesus as much as I did. I did meet him. It's hard to put into words the feelings that I felt when I knew I had found "the one;" the one who loved me for me was willing to fight for me, and wanted to spend his life with me. The dreams I had dreamed were finally coming true. I graduated from Bible college and six months later, I would be getting married. Pinch me. "MRS." degree complete.

Those of you who are married and have children know that it is a journey not for the faint of heart. There are highs and lows, and higher highs, and sometimes the lowest of lows. That came for me after thirteen years of marriage.

Divorce; the "D" word; the thing I said would never happen to me. To say that the rug of my life was ripped out from under me would be an understatement. This was definitely NOT part of the plan for my life. I mean, we have two sons. Where will we live? How will my heart ever heal from the most devastating rejection I have ever known? I remember the pain being worse than any sickness I had ever had. I couldn't take a pill to make this pain go away. I remember being so glad when it was time to go to sleep at night, so I could finally turn off my mind and all the pain, but then the morning would come, and it would start all over again. I knew the Lord loved me completely and would take care of us, but the grief over the death of the dream for my life was unbearable.

During that time, my mom sent a cassette tape with a teaching on it that has forever been engrained on my mind.

The pastor was talking about how we weather the storms that come to pass in our lives. The key words he used were, "get bitter or get better; the choice is yours." As painful as this part of my life was, I knew that my number one priority was and would always be my sons. I knew that the last thing I wanted for them was to be raised by a bitter mother. So, from that moment, I chose to get better.

Their dad was as constant in their lives as he could be. He was consistent in his time with them as well as always taking care of his financial responsibilities. I chose to continue to make him a hero to our boys because I never wanted them to harbor anger in their hearts toward him. The issues in our marriage were ours to deal with, not theirs. He and I were able to maintain a good relationship, and for that I was grateful.

The spiritual meaning of *grace* is, "The divine influence which operates in humans to regenerate and sanctify, to inspire virtuous impulses, and to impart strength to endure trial and resist temptation; and as an individual virtue or excellence of divine origin." I felt like I knew what grace was up to that point, but when I became a single mom, grace became personified to me. Grace was my friend, my constant companion, my mentor, my guide, my wisdom, and my strength. It wasn't some spiritual "Christianese" word that I had heard all of my life. It was now a part of me, down to the marrow of my bones. I could not look to anyone else to carry me through this phase of my life. Don't get me wrong, I had an amazing group of people holding my arms up during this battle (Exodus 17:12-14), but the ultimate responsibility of the raising of my sons and the attitude of my heart while doing it was up to me. But as a pastor recently said, "What do you do when your situation is screaming louder than your inner faith?" (Dustin Bates, Church Eleven32)

Thankfully, I was able to work in a Christian school, and my sons were able to attend tuition-free. God had us planted in exactly the right place with exactly the right people. I took on additional jobs after school in order to help with our financial condition. God always provided. Always. When I look back, I am completely amazed at how we made it. Gas money would be needed, and that day in the mail, there would be a letter from my parents with G.A.M.M. (Gas and Milk Money) inside. We didn't have extras. No internet, cable, or big televisions. Birthday and Christmas gifts were certainly not extravagant by any means, but the boys always got blessed as well from other family members. I would sometimes cry to myself, thinking about how we could not take vacations or how there was not much money for extras. I would apologize to them, but they never once complained or became ungrateful for what they had. God was working in their lives, and creating true gratitude, as well as the ability to pray and trust in Him for provision.

I'll never forget one evening when the boys and I were driving to a movie. I began to quietly cry as I was driving. I was thinking about the fact that I no longer had my husband to sit by me in a movie and hold my hand or to go on family outings together. My oldest son heard me sniffing, and he reached his hand out and put it on my shoulder and said, "It's okay, Mom, I will take care of you." What a precious moment. I looked at him and said, "Thank you bud, but I know God will take care of all of us."

I honestly do not know how people can go through this type of life-altering trauma without knowing the Lord. There were so many times that I cried out in anger to God, asking how this could be happening to me, the one who had been faithfully serving Him the majority of my life. I could feel His arms picking me up and holding me during those times. He was not mad at me for the legitimate feelings I had. Instead, He let me know that He was and would always be there for us.

I became stronger. Not because of anything I did in my own strength, but because of my complete dependence upon Him. My sons saw that. They saw a mom with an unwavering faith, regardless of the circumstances surrounding us. Did they see a mom who would get upset, cry, yell, repent... then repeat? Yes, they did. A lot. But one of the best things we can do for our children is to let them see our humanity. They can know that we make mistakes, but they can also see that we pick ourselves back up, ask for forgiveness, and move on; making every effort to not make the same mistakes again.

Now, I am definitely no expert on raising children. I could list a million and one things that I wish I would have done differently. But I can tell you what has made the biggest difference for us. Prayer. Lots and lots of it. I have seen my young boys who loved Jesus grow to be men who love Jesus.

From a very young age, I taught my sons to pray. Pray about everything! Have a test at school? Let's pray. Fell down on the concrete and skinned their knees? Let's pray and ask Jesus to heal. Someone at school was picking on them. Let's pray for them because they are probably hurting too. Nothing was off-limits. Nothing was too small or too big. Prayers did not have to be only at night before bed, but they became a habit for us as we drove to school, before we ate, when we were leaving on a trip, when we were with someone who was sick, when we were sad, when there was disobedience and consequences, and so much more. Prayers did not have to be long and drawn out. Sometimes they could just be, "Help me, Jesus." Sometimes they were just saying "Thank you, Jesus."

Imagine if there were only certain times each day that children could talk to their parents. What a horrible restriction that would be! Are we doing the same thing in creating a tangible image of Father God to our children if they only see us pray at certain times? Our children mimic what they see us do. If they see us praying and worshipping our Heavenly Father in a way that is unencumbered and free, then they too will feel the freedom to pray and worship in that way.

I am beyond blessed that my two sons have now grown into awesome men of God. I am in awe when I look at these men, my boys, who have matured and recognized their need for a Savior and are fully unashamed of the Gospel of Jesus Christ. They live their lives so that others can truly see and know the love of God.

My oldest son and my beautiful daughter-in-love have given me three amazing, perfect grandsons who have completely stolen my heart. I now have a chance to invest in their lives as their Lolli. What an amazing privilege I have been given in this life. My Father trusted me enough to give me sons to raise, and now the blessings continue to the next generation.

There is a prayer that I prayed over my sons each night as they went to bed, and now, I am blessed to be able to pray that prayer over my grandsons:

*"Father, I thank you for raising _____ up to be a mighty man of God; full of knowledge, wisdom, understanding, integrity, faithfulness, commitment, loyalty, and purity all the days of his life."*

I added more to that prayer to make it specific to each child. It is so important to pray for the things your child feels are important, so they can develop their trust in a Heavenly Father who truly cares about all of their desires.

Do I completely understand all that has happened in my life to bring me to this point? Absolutely not. In fact, if I dwell too much on what has been, it is like driving while only looking through the rearview mirror. There is a reason the windshield is bigger. The rearview mirror is important for glancing back, but if we keep looking at it while we drive, we will not only hurt ourselves but those around us. Everything that I have gone through has made me the woman of God that I am today. It has made my sons the men of God they are today. I cannot go back and change anything that has happened, but I can be confident in knowing that I am held in the very center of God's hand; past, present, and future. His plan is best. Every. Single. Time.

*Chapter 11*

# IT ISN'T ABOUT THE STRUGGLE, IT'S ABOUT THE VICTORY

**By Melinda McGlasson**

My name is Melinda McGlasson and I am a proud Texhoma, Oklahoma resident, and I teach choir for the Texhoma School. I am also the wife of Dallas McGlasson and mother of Isaiah, Grayson, and Blake. Together, we pastor Connection Church in Guymon, OK. In 2016, I signed as an International Christian Recording artist with Creative Soul Records and McLaughlin Music Group based in Nashville, TN. My first international album was released in 2016 and is played in 47 different countries. I have had the opportunity to appear on globally televised shows such as TBN and Hour of Power, as well as appearances in various Christian magazines. I released a single to radio in October 2017. My number one hit songs on the Christian Chart are

"My Deliverer" and "Trust Him." You can find more information about my singing ministry at <u>melindamcglasson.com</u>

Life is a funny thing. It is full of ups and downs, and sometimes it seems as though you are in a dream. Reality sinks in and you realize that you must face whatever good or bad comes your way. You can always plan ahead for a celebration or for doomsday, but no matter how much you plan, you will never know exactly how you will react until that day comes. The truth of the matter is when life gives you lemons what will you do with them?

It was a hot, humid summer in two thousand fifteen. We did what we do every summer in July, we went as a family to Church camp. I swam, played volleyball, softball, and hiked like I always have done every year. Getting ready for the evening service I noticed a pain in my right side. I sat on the edge of the bed and thought it was strange, but knew it would pass. I had taken several crazy falls that afternoon playing sand volleyball, so I thought to myself that must be where the pain came from. I took some inflammatory meds and went to church. The next morning, we headed home. We had a wonderful time and was prepping for the camp video that I typically put together for Sunday morning as the campers shared their testimonies.

Ah, the weekend is here! It's Saturday morning, and I have a list of things I would like to accomplish from being gone a whole week. I sit up in my bed, stand up to start my day, and I quickly sit back down.

The same pain on my right side is back! This time, it comes with stomachaches. I tell my husband, Dallas, that I must have picked up a stomach bug or something. He encourages me to rest; telling me that the week's worth of camp laundry could wait. "There goes my plans," I think to myself.

Sunday morning arrives, and I get up to start my day, ready to go lead people in worship. As I am getting dressed, the pain comes back. What could this be? Is it my appendix? Should I go to the hospital? Will it pass eventually? I sit down on the bed, trying not to become sick, the pain intensifies, and I then realize something is definitely not right in my body, and I would need to go to the hospital. Not thinking anything was majorly wrong, I encouraged Dallas to go ahead and go to church, as he was the senior pastor, and I would keep him updated. I knew I would probably be there all morning, so there was no sense him sitting around waiting.

After running several tests, the ER doctor comes in and says that I would need to see an OBGYN doctor within twenty-four hours. "Doctor, what is the urgency?" He replies, "It appears that you have a septated ovarian tumor on your right ovary measuring the size of a large grapefruit." The doctor then tells me to rest and not to bend or squat. I obeyed the doctor's orders, and was scheduled to be seen by a local OBGYN on Monday morning.

Still not thinking anything was horribly wrong, I went to the appointment by myself, and I told my family that I would keep them posted as to what the doctor said. The pain had actually subsided with some help of medication given by the ER doctor. As I was sitting in the room waiting for the doctor, all I could think of was how things can change so quickly, when just a week ago at that same time, I was headed to go encounter the Lord at a church camp, and now I sit waiting for a doctor to explain what a septated tumor was. Crazy!

The doctor walks in. She looks down at the papers, reviewing what the hospital has sent over, and she sits down. No "Hello." No "How are you today?" She says, "Wow, you're so young." Normally I would be flattered, but her tear-filled eyes quickly got my attention. What could this be? Is something so wrong that everyone is afraid to be straightforward with me? What? Just tell me! Seeing the concern in my eyes, she says, "I am just a traveling OB doctor coming through the area, but we need to get you to an oncologist who specializes in OB. Do you have a preference?" I responded to her with concern and almost sarcasm, "Ma'am I do not even have an OB doctor, let alone an oncologist. Can you just tell me what is going on?" She explained in depth what a septated ovarian tumor was. She showed me my ultrasound, and spent a long while in the room with me, helping me to fully understand what the radiologist had found. She hugged me! She told me that I would need to go back over to the hospital and get a blood test to test for cancer.

I left that office in disbelief. What was happening? Was I not just praising the Lord, and leading people before Him a week ago, and now this? I began to cry, and I called my husband and told him what was happening. He and I thought it was a routine checkup; nothing to be concerned about. My mind began to travel through the seven stages of worry. I did not know what was going to happen, but I knew wisdom was telling me to get a handle on things quickly.

Tuesday morning comes, and I feel led to contact another OBGYN doctor forty miles away from my town. "Good morning, Doctor's office, can I help you?" "Yes, this is Melinda McGlasson, and I need to be seen as soon as possible!" She replies, "Ma'am, what is your date of birth? Our next available time is next Wednesday." I then reply, "Can you see if a doctor's office contacted you about me?" She comes back, "No ma'am, they have not, but when they do, we can let you know." Their closest opening was seven days from now. Maybe this was not the place to go? I just felt so strongly I was to see this OBGYN, so I said, "Yes, make me that appointment."

Wednesday morning came. My phone rings. "Mrs. McGlasson, the doctor read your report, and he would like to see you as soon as possible!" For a moment, it felt like my heart stopped. What could be so wrong? I went to that appointment and the doctor confirmed that I would need to have the mass removed. He told me that he would help me, however he could, past the surgery and point me in the right direction to find the best oncologist that he knows and trusts. Was this a dream? Would someone please wake me up and tell me it was all just a bad dream?

In those moments, I had the opportunity to rise in my faith or fall in my fear. I chose to rise above! The night before my surgery, I stood for two hours leading our church in a night of worship. I worshipped while I waited for my healing! I remember feeling energized while I was leading worship that night. I had no pain, no worries, no fears. I only focused on worshipping Him. When I went into my surgery, I knew that the Lord had healed me. He, in fact, did! The pathology reports came back clear. I finally had total peace once again.

Fast forward three months later, November of two thousand fifteen, and I sat in yet another oncology office with news that I would need to have a total thyroidectomy. That pathology report came back with a different diagnosis than my previous report. I was told that I had stage three thyroid cancer. At this point in my walk, I was not as strong physically, emotionally, and spiritually. I was tired! I wasn't sure what was going to happen, and I wasn't sure if I had the fight in me to go forward.

Sometimes at your lowest moments, you find who you are made of, and you also begin to see things in a whole new perspective. I had faced two major battles within two months from one another. I had seen the Lord miraculously heal me, and had seen His provision by using a doctor to bring healing. Not for a moment did I feel like the Lord had left me, but that does not negate the fact that I was exhausted in all areas of my life. I believe that sometimes you are strong enough to stand on your own, and sometimes you need others to hold you up so that you can stand. I am so thankful that I had my family, church, and friends to encourage me.

During those weakened moments came some of my strongest songs. I learned to hear the voice of Jesus over the doctor's reports. I also learned to see others in a whole new light.

In January two thousand sixteen, I was not only declared cancer-free, but I signed a record deal with a Christian recording company. The label and I were able to produce ten of the songs I wrote during my tough season, and compiled them onto a cd. The Lord was continuing to prove Himself as faithful and true. The opportunity came in two thousand eighteen for me to produce another album, where my music would now become known on a global platform. Another opportunity came for me to be on Trinity Broadcast Network, Hour of Power, and on radio stations around the world. Look at the Lord! He continues to use my trials to bring hope and healing to others.

Yes, I am now declared cancer-free, but it is a fight every day to keep my mind and heart attuned to His voice and will for my life. James chapter one tells us that we will face trials and tribulations, so this gives me a forecast that I will face things in my future, so I must prepare now to praise Him no matter what those trials and tribulations are.

Every day we are each faced with a choice to continue or to give up. Jesus does not promise to pick you up and carry you away from the storm, He promises to walk with you through the storm. The Lord has given us a resilience to stand against whatever may come our way. I believe that both of these circumstances helped me to become the woman I am today, but it is even bigger than me. It is meant to help others! If I can go through hardships and come out of them praising God, and willing to be transparent in my weaknesses, that gives others a hope that they, too, can go through anything they face. It isn't about the struggle, it's about the victory!

# Chapter 12

# THE BEAUTY OF ASHES

### By Fallon Lee

My name is Fallon Danae Lee, and I am a current resident of the Dallas area, a stay-at-home mom to our three beautiful boys, and married to my best friend. I graduated from Baylor University with a degree in cultural anthropology, with a focus in poverty studies, and now I find my passion in holistic health, nutrition science, home church, pursuing community, and connecting with and ministering to others with chronic illness.

If you would have told me as a relatively healthy, extremely active teenager I would grow up to not only develop a chronic illness, but also bear a child with puzzling medical conditions, I would have never believed you. If you would have told me God would eventually strip away one of the things in which I held the most confidence, my health, and the health of my children, I doubt I would think you any less than crazy. Sure, I had asthma, occasional migraines, and some anxiety as a child and young adult, but those things seemed relatively normal at that point in time. Little did I know, my son and I would eventually both be diagnosed with life-long, difficult illnesses, which would lead to the most heart-wrenching years of my life.

In July 2015, I gave birth via cesarean to my second beautiful baby boy. I had what would be considered a low-risk pregnancy, but was admitted to the hospital about a month prior to delivery for memory loss, an atypical migraine, and vision issues. I remember playing games with my family one moment, feeling a little odd the next, and soon had lost the ability to verbalize any coherent thoughts, including remembering my soon-to-be-born son's name. We rushed to the nearest emergency room, and after a few standard tests, determined the issue unnamable and a mere fluke. We chalked it up to stress, and all but forgot about it, although I knew something was not right. In all honesty, I had been feeling like something was not quite right in my body over the last several years after experiencing symptoms such as crippling anxiety and bouts of depression, which were both often written off as a lack of faith. I persevered in my Scripture reading, praying, and crying out to the Lord during these dark times, wondering if my devotion was not strong enough to save me from these evils, and frequently concluding that to be the truth. As many women experience during the postpartum period, these issues only grew stronger after the birth of my son. Having a second child was, of course, one of the most precious gifts I could ever receive, but as many mothers discover, the months following delivery can be quite a mental and physical battle.

When my gorgeous happy boy was just two months old, I started noticing odd rashes and stomach issues, which led me to consult his pediatrician. His doctor immediately recognized these symptoms as frequently linked to a dairy allergy, and urged me as a breastfeeding mother to eliminate all milk products from my diet. It certainly helped, as difficult as I found it at the time, but his issues gradually continued to worsen. We pursued allergy testing, which came back more severe than I could ever imagine–my tiny boy was allergic to around ten food items and countless environmental substances, and we prayed the removal of these things would improve his skin, which seemed to be worsening daily. He was now covered with rashes, determined to be eczema, that we could not seem to get under control. We pursued all the best dermatologists and doctors, who each insisted on a specific regimen of products, steroids, and care that would cause him to improve. As someone who hardly knew the correct spelling of "eczema" (and had many internet searches with all sorts of incorrect versions of the word), I felt completely at a loss on what to do. I continued to heed the advice of the medical professionals we were seeing while suppressing a strong feeling we had not yet found the right solution. I could not shake the feeling food, chemicals, my own poor health, and a reaction to vaccinations were at play, although I struggled to find a health professional who would confirm my persuasions. We spent nearly half a year cycling through doctors, new lotions, different steroids, various bath routines, all to no avail–if we were lucky, we would see a few days of improvement, but the eczema would come back with a vengeance. I find it nearly impossible to verbalize the emotions I felt over the course of these months or describe the state of my son's body and skin. I was angry at the Lord, frustrated with the medical community, and burdened by my lack of control as a mother. I cried every day over my precious son's misery– he scratched constantly, he sat languid on his playmat, covered in weeping sores, in too much pain to attempt to move. I couldn't find a clear spot on his tiny face to kiss. He struggled to sleep, and would often wake up bloody from trying, fruitlessly, to alleviate some of his itchiness throughout the night. His development began to slow, leaving him behind other children his age, and my fear for his well-being grew daily. Every single health professional we saw declared his case of eczema the worst they had ever seen. I begged and pleaded with the Lord to give us an answer and to remove my poor baby's misery, but we continued to sit helplessly in the throngs of sickness, pain, and confusion. Anger and bitterness grew in my heart like weeds, because for one of the first times in my life, I was faced with a problem I could not answer or explain. I felt as if God were distant, unconcerned, merely watching as we struggled helplessly. My head knew the character of God, but my heart could not seem to find it.

In the midst of this season, my own health continued to worsen. My needs had been put on the back burner in pursuit of healing for my son, but it eventually became apparent I needed to find answers and a diagnosis as well. I began to see various professionals in the hopes of finding an answer to my hospital scare during pregnancy, as well as my current symptoms. I saw neurologists, had MRIs, and went down several fruitless pathways. Finally, my primary care doctor discovered I had an autoimmune disease called Hashimoto's thyroiditis, which had left my body barely functioning, but according to the doctor, could not be cured or treated much more than offering life-long medication. The news stung. It would have to wait, however. I continued to live with overwhelming anxiety, depression, back and joint pain, migraines, numbness in my extremities, insomnia, fatigue, heart palpitations, chest pain, shortness of breath, and many other symptoms. I wanted to find healing, of course, but my son needed it more.

In December of that year, at just six months old, my son was admitted to the hospital for an eczema infection and breathing trouble. His skin was the worst we had ever seen it. His doctor had recently recommended we switch to an incredibly pricey allergy-friendly formula instead of breastfeeding in the hopes it would help. My son had grown increasingly worse on the formula, but the formula company, doctors, and other professionals all assured us the formula itself could not be the issue. The medical staff on rotation was baffled at his condition; they affirmed we were doing all the right things, using the recommended products, and seeking the suggested treatment. I finally felt brave enough to offer up the idea of food being a culprit in part, even past the allergens we had already removed–I had already started to notice a greater connection, beyond just dairy, between his eczema and things he, or I, was eating–but all the doctors, dermatologists, and breathing specialists we had seen (both past and present) were adamant food was not the issue. We spent three days in the hospital, during which our community was relentlessly praying on our behalf. A friend from church who had experienced chronic health issues herself stopped by the hospital to give me a few books on the impact of food on autoimmune and other recurring health issues, including a book on the Whole 30 program and the Autoimmune Paleo diet. I was only vaguely familiar with these regimens, but immediately felt the Lord leading me to pursue this route. We were released from the hospital on Christmas Eve, and headed back home with a happier baby, whose skin had cleared from the steroids he was given, and whose breathing had regulated from the treatments. I was overjoyed to be leaving with a seemingly healed little boy, but knew deep down our journey was far from over.

Within barely a week, the eczema started creeping back in; all the feelings of peace, gratefulness, and calm from seeing a little boy with clear skin had vanished, and we were left right back in the confused state to which we were so accustomed. "Why, God?" I wondered. Why would He let us experience false healing, just to have the world come crashing back down? Somehow, I knew pursuing healing through whole foods, gut-healing, and holistic remedies was the right next step. I decided to resume breastfeeding, and the switch away from formula allowed us to see an immediate improvement; while that was encouraging, it now meant there was not a single formula on the market that would work for my son. I would have to discover his food sensitivities and alter my own diet to fit them. I dove into an autoimmune version of the Paleo diet, which was scientifically formulated to remove foods that could potentially be inflammatory for individuals with chronic health issues, and I prioritized focusing on the most nutrient-dense food options available. Somehow, it seemed both far-fetched and sensible all at once. Additionally, we started switching all of our little one's products, our cleaning supplies, and all household beauty and care items to include only nontoxic ingredients, instead of simply "fragrance-free," as had been recommended but had not proven helpful. We continued to pursue more internal healing, finally convinced that addressing gut health was more important than mere external approaches, and continued to use eliminations, food diaries, and alternative medical treatments to identify food triggers.

We saw slow but steady improvement. Contrary to treatments we had been using, which would offer fast but short-lived healing, the holistic approach we had chosen would take time, commitment, trial and error, and endless amounts of patience. The healing would be more gradual, but long lasting. As I sat at my computer one day, recounting all my little one had been through, I realized the Hashimoto's symptoms I had been experiencing had drastically improved and nearly disappeared, after just one month of following the Autoimmune Paleo diet. Even though I had chosen to start this protocol for my still-nursing child, God had graciously used it to begin bringing healing to us both. In that moment, I was reminded I was not forgotten. In the midst of running relentlessly after healing for my child, my heavenly Father was doing the same for me. He cared even more deeply for my son and for me than I ever could.

During our suffering, we found support from our community like we could never have imagined or anticipated. We would find envelopes of cash in our mailbox to help us cover our growing medical bills; we had a sweet family purchase us a brand-new washing machine when ours gave out, some of our dear friends gave us one of their cars when my husband's bit the dust; never in my life had I felt so honored and cared for. We had a team of people praying constantly, always making sure our physical needs were met, and lavishing us with enough grace to encourage us to keep fighting. Through our kind friends and family trying all they could to connect us with others who had similar journeys, I began to receive online support from people I had never met, but who had committed to praying for us as well. I eventually connected with several mothers who had also watched their little ones suffer from eczema, food allergies, and overall immune system issues, one of which pointed us to an international eczema doctor. The man, Dr. Aron, practiced out of South Africa, but prescribed what seemed to be a compounded "miracle cream" worldwide. It sounded highly sketchy at best. I kept the idea in the back of my mind, and we pressed on pursuing healing the best we knew how.

My own health continued to waver, and despite feeling generally better, my body was growing increasingly more sensitive to certain foods and other triggers for reasons we struggled to identify. I found myself unable to eat more than about 20 foods, between my nursing son's food intolerances and my own, and I began to rapidly lose weight. I remember crying when I saw pictures of myself because I looked so thin–and I felt malnourished and underfed, with no options. I did not have the option to stop breastfeeding my son, as he was still not yet a year old, and we could not manage to find a formula or alternative that did not make him worse. I knew the decision to continue nursing was right for us, but it was incredibly difficult. I began to grow tired in my spirit, my body, and mind. I grew increasingly more tired of explaining myself to people, while feeling like they could not possibly understand why we chose this route. I was tired of not being able to eat out or have friends bring food over on a hard day. I was tired of every meeting, gathering, function, and party being centered around food we could not have. I was tired of both my son and I being so limited in our diets we could not take most of the supplements we had been prescribed, because our bodies were so in shambles they failed to process basic vitamins and minerals. I was tired of pouring money into new tests and appointments to get more answers we desperately needed, tired of seeing my child suffer, tired of thinking about all the ways my son was currently deprived and would continue to be deprived, made fun of, or left out in the future, tired of hearing another story of someone who was healed easily through the steps we had already taken, and tired of the things we had been doing for so long working quickly for others on our same journey. Most days, I had no idea where my energy for the next day would come from. Too little food, too many tears, and too few good nights of sleep left my entire body feeling unable to keep persevering. I wept with my family, my community, and my husband, but I truly felt as if nobody could understand the weight I carried. Despite the improvement my son and I had seen, I felt suffocated by the finality of it all. "Eczema couldn't be cured," everyone said, just managed. "Autoimmune diseases never heal," I heard repeatedly. This was our portion in life, and I genuinely had no idea how we could continue to live this way. The two of us were on the worse end of the spectrum for our respective illnesses, and nobody could seem to explain why we were not seeing more healing. I grew frustrated over pouring so much energy into mine and my son's health. I felt I was missing out on greater kingdom work; I wanted energy to serve others more. I wanted the time and physical capability to be more present in my community. I wanted to have an excess in my bank account to give to others, instead of pouring it into our health expenses. I wanted the anger growing in my heart to subside, but the Lord kept us where we were, and I had to trust He would somehow redeem our sorrows, to trust He would be faithful to let us see the fruit of our labors, even when the labor seemed so irrelevant. I prayed more than leading people to physical healing, our story would draw people to Jesus, and while having no idea how that would pan out, I had to trust the Lord would not waste the energy, time, and resources we had put into getting better.

We finally chose to consult the international eczema doctor recommended to us. I submitted our information with much trepidation, mingled with hopefulness, praying this would not be another waste of time and money. We anxiously waited for the cream to arrive, knowing when it did, we could use it to help soothe our son's skin enough to help us more easily determine triggers. When it came, it was all it was praised to be. We saw an overnight improvement in our son's skin–he slept the first night after we applied the cream, and his skin looked more beautiful and clearer with every passing day. I felt like a teenager attempting (and badly failing) to guard my heart over it all–I could hardly believe it! The eczema healing we had pleaded for, wept for, was finally here. Over the course of the next several months, my baby boy went from miserable, limp, and covered in sores to a happy child with almost entirely clear skin. I will never forget taking him to a playground not long after starting the cream and pushing him in an infant swing while I watched him smile and giggle for the first time in as long as I could remember. I remember the tears of joy I shed that day, mingled with the weight of the grief I had carried, over seeing my little one feeling well enough to laugh. At that moment, I decided it was finally okay for me to let the feelings of hope and happiness flood my spirit, the feelings I had been fighting hard to suppress in case things worsened again, and I let myself revel in the improvement we had finally found. I watched over the next several weeks as my baby began to actually play, babble, gain weight, sleep well, and find healing. His skin was still not perfect, but he was starting to thrive for the first time in his short life. At this point, he was still nursing, and our diets remained incredibly limited, but I found strength in the victory of seeing his skin improve.

Within a few short months, our precious but difficult breast-feeding journey came to an end, which made identifying food triggers exponentially easier and subsequently led to further skin improvement. I began to gain weight back that I desperately needed, finally being able to eat several items my son reacted to, and the peaceful season for which we had so desperately longed finally arrived. We spent several blissful months witnessing continued improvement in my son's skin and overall health, and my own health remained in a stable enough place to see progress as well.

Every calm has an end unfortunately, and soon my son was having fairly consistent breathing issues, along with my own autoimmune symptoms coming back in full force. We felt as if we were constantly paying medical debt, as my little one was in and out of the hospital and emergency room quite frequently for breathing treatments, and as I was finally pursuing further help and healing for myself. Through a series of blood tests with my phenomenal functional medicine team, we discovered there was a source of mold somewhere in our rental home; that, combined with my increasing chemical sensitivities and side business involving paints, stains, and other harmful substances, had made my body begin to spiral out of control again. Thankfully, our lease ended not long after we discovered this news and the Lord provided us with a beautiful home beyond what we expected. Despite the healing my son and I had already found, I still felt like we struggled to get our heads above water. We could not seem to find an exact answer for why my own health issues continued to worsen, and we lived in a perpetual state of fear over the allergies my son has. We had found hope, certainly, but I often had to force my spirit to remember the grace God had given us.

A couple of years down the road, I am incredibly grateful to say we have both found more healing. My son's skin is always clear, except for exposure to his triggers, he rarely has breathing issues, and he is the most joyful little boy who ever lived (my own, unbiased opinion). My own health has greatly improved after finding the perfect balance of programs, doctors, and supplements. We continue to focus on foods with the most nutrients, and must avoid several ingredients; we steer clear of toxic products and substances, and we have kept pursuing medical treatment through the naturopathic community. I genuinely feel as if our quality of life is as good as anyone's with chronic illness, praise God. We have watched the Lord lead us to treatments and methods which defy the medical community's thoughts at large—nobody ever thought my son would heal from his eczema or that I would lead a symptom-free life as someone with an autoimmune disease, but by God's mercy, we are both thriving. As painful as it is to recount the darkest days of my life, where I watched my son suffer more than I felt I could bear, it is a beautiful reminder of Jesus' faithfulness to us. I have learned more about trials, about trusting in the Lord, and about destroying my own idols over the course of these painful years than ever in my life, and I have witnessed the community of believers around us act as the hands and feet of Christ like nothing I have ever experienced.

I truly believe the most important part of our story is this: it is not finished. We have not achieved perfect health. My son still has several life-threatening allergies, some immune system issues, and chemical sensitivities that will probably keep him from attending school outside of the home. Neither of us have the freedom to eat at many restaurants, consume food cooked outside of our home, or eat anything without a detailed ingredient list. I am still fighting to find more answers and more healing for both of our bodies, but somehow, I find immense beauty in this unfinalized picture, because it continues to force me into a constant state of dependence on Jesus. I may never see complete healing for my son or for myself on this earth, but I can rest daily in the fact that because of my beautiful Savior, my soul and spirit are untarnished. My son and I will one day stand in the presence of our Father, perfectly whole, completely healed, utterly pain-free. Quite frankly, I have no idea what the remainder of our lives will look like. I have no assurances that either of us will continue to improve, but I have confidence in serving a God who is never surprised and never defeated.

There was a time in my life where I genuinely believed I did not want suffering. I'm not sure any of us, outside of a biblical perspective, want to go through seasons of hurt, but the more I study the Word of God, the deeper appreciation I have for trials. The more I spend time with Jesus, and with His saints, the greater understanding I have for why life cannot, and should not, be easy. One of the pillars of my faith during these years of hardship have been verses like Philippians 1:29, "For it has been granted to you that for the sake of Christ you should not only believe in him but also suffer for his sake" (ESV). To me, the most beautiful words in this verse are that we have been "granted" to suffer. The confusing, yet awe-inspiring truth exists that while suffering entered the world because of sin and the fall, God, in His kindness and sovereignty, still uses it for the ultimate good of His people. I can't think of anything more comforting in a world so full of hurt. Not only does Jesus gift us with this honor of suffering as He did, but it ultimately brings glory to His name when His children suffer well. I pray I do not forget this simple truth: even if God had never brought any healing to my family, He still would be righteous and good. There exists some confusion, and danger, when we begin to think God owes us healing or redemption this side of eternity. As I think back on these dark years, there were truly times I felt as if God should heal my son or myself because we deserved it, and I think that was more dangerous than any life-threatening illness; these feelings proved in part why the anger in my heart continued to grow during this season. If nothing else, illness has taught me about the utter holiness of God in a way nothing else could have.

I am thankful to say my family is currently expecting our third little boy, a true gift from the Father. While my husband and I were uncertain whether we would continue bearing biological children due to my own health issues and bad genetics, God granted us new life while we still lived in fear. Not long before we discovered the pregnancy, a call with my dear Papa (whom the rest of you know as Jim Jamieson) left me with a clear picture from the Lord to anticipate even more healing. He recounted a very vivid dream he had, where I was weeping over carrying an unbearable burden, and as he felt the Lord reveal to him at the time, that I was "pregnant" with the weight of it all. He felt God expounding on this metaphor, as we believed it to be at the time, explaining how I would experience the pains of childbirth and would find healing on the other side. It was a beautiful, tear-inducing, encouraging picture, but as I was not expecting a child at the time, we thought it nothing more than mere imagery. A few months later, a confirmed pregnancy reminded me of these words. I felt too overwhelmed and unsure of whether God actually intended them for my pregnancy; after all, my doctors agree, two virtually back-to-back pregnancies (9 months apart) is part of what caused my body to continue breaking down as it had; women with autoimmune issues can often experience a major decline in health following the birth of a child. Suffice it to say, this dream, while hopeful, seemed to make little sense in light of what we know about chronic illness and pregnancy, but for some reason, God continues to perpetuate this idea of healing in both my own thoughts and those around me. A conversation with my mother-in-law (who is also penning a chapter of this book) revealed that she too felt strongly God would somehow use this baby and this pregnancy to bring my body further healing. As we have recently begun the process of choosing a name for our new little one, we found ourselves struggling to choose a fitting middle name. My mother-in-law was driving home one evening when she repeatedly had a single name come to mind; she could not shake it, despite it being relatively uncommon and not something we had been considering. When she looked into the meaning, she found it meant "Jehovah has healed." I could hardly believe it. Needless to say, "Josiah" fit perfectly with the first name we had chosen, "Bennett." Hope and excitement fill my heart over this pregnancy and this baby, and I can hardly wait to see what God brings to fulfillment after his birth.

God continues to teach me that while there are practical steps He has placed in our path to bring healing to both my son and me, He is ultimately in control of our bodies and our betterment. While I have no idea how this further healing will pan out, the Lord continues to remind me it is possible against all odds. Jesus continues to patiently and gently remove the bitterness that festered in me during these difficult years, and constantly shows me even sin can be redeemed by a sovereign God–nothing is outside of His domain. I would be remiss if I did not dive deeper, not only into the situational darkness we faced during these past years, but also the spiritual, and while I have referenced the state of my heart in this period, the topic begs for more attention. Anyone who has been married and had children will confidently tell you few things sanctify and expose your own pride and sinfulness like these two events, and while I firmly believed that concept, I still had a decent amount of confidence in my own patient abilities after a couple of years of marriage and parenthood. As my second son was born and we were thrust deeper into the reality of suffering, I found myself saying and thinking I had suddenly become an angry person as a result of my situation. It had not been common to my character up until this point to lash out in frustration or to feel overly consumed by madness in any form, and the lie I told myself for a while was that I had turned into an anger-filled woman because of my circumstances, not because of my heart. I thought if God would only answer my prayer and bring us healing, the anger in my heart would dissipate, and I would return to my former patient state. The Lord was gracious to me; my sin did not immediately disappear, but I learned a lesson far greater by walking through it; it was not that anger and entitlement did not exist in me before, it simply had not been brought to the light yet. If I am carrying a cup full of orange juice and somebody bumps into me and spills it, the bump did not create what was inside the cup as much as it revealed it. While I walked through something that tested and stretched every limit in my being–spiritual, physical, emotional–the deepest parts of my heart began to show, and what I found was not an unwavering trust in who God was, but bitterness and self-righteousness over the path I thought He should have given me. I realized, for most of my life, until this point, I was accustomed to being easily angered over the sin in other's lives, but not the sin in my own. I was quick to place blame on my surroundings and my circumstances instead of owning the shocking reality of my fleshly desire toward self-reliance and control. As I began to realize the darkness living in me, I tried to alleviate my sin through confession, prayer, and Scripture reading–all the practices I had been taught to combat sin, yet none of them seemed to pull me out of my shame-filled hole. The sad truth is, though, I was embarking on a daily battle against our physical suffering while treating my true enemy like an inconvenience rather than a monster. While my anger began to reveal itself as a direct response to my situation, it began to take root and attack my family through bitter words, extreme impatience, and a severe lack of grace toward those I loved most. I eventually began to grow hateful toward myself as well, desperately desiring to see this wickedness taken from me, and further frustrated at God for not rescuing me out of my chains.

As is true with the rest of my story, God is still working, and while I remain on this earth, my sin has not yet disappeared. Yes, Jesus has been gracious to constantly pursue me and forgive me, but I truly believe my own heart's darkness has revealed a necessary truth: without sin, I have no need for a Savior, and while God is utterly holy and deeply hates sin, He is still powerful enough to redeem what is broken and meant for evil. When my life as I knew it was stripped away—my health, my control, any righteous qualities I thought I possessed—and all I had left was Jesus; I found He was all I needed. He still continues to teach me this lesson and daily reminds me of the grace He offers. I truly believe I felt stuck in my shortcomings for so long because my eyes were continuing to turn inward; I kept focusing on the wretched state of my heart instead of on the forgiveness and grace Jesus offered me. God revealed to me that continuing to walk in self-condemnation was another form of my own pride because Jesus is the only one who has the authority and final word over my sin, and He does not condemn me. While I still live in hatred of my sin, my Father continues to gently lift my eyes to Jesus on the Cross, where all of it was forgiven.

Even while my spirit can tend to lean toward hopelessness and shame, Jesus has already paid my debt in full, and will continue to lead me toward sanctification and redemption until the day He returns. I long for that day, truly, in a way I never could have without experiencing the pains of chronic illness in my family and the heart revelation it brought in the process, and I find peace in confidently saying this path is still the one I would choose if I had the ability to turn back time. I would do it all over again for the sake of God's glory being proclaimed in my own heart and in the hearts of those around me. I pray as you take in my story, dear reader, God leads you to an acknowledgment of the beauty of His sacrifice, even in light of your own failures, like you have never before experienced, and that we will one day soon give a glad farewell to pain, sickness, and darkness, and stand before Him face-to-face as pure, unblemished, awe-struck beings.

# My Look at America from the Viewpoint of an Ordinary American Citizen

**by Jim Jamieson**

S haring my viewpoints as an ordinary American citizen is certainly going to be different than many viewpoints we hear in the news media or social media in the past few years; so many opinions, not only of anger, but also hatred towards people of all backgrounds and social status. Some might be justified; it's according to whom you talk to or give a listening ear. We all get somewhat upset when we point out or see individuals who have an agenda to bring destruction to the future, which belongs to our coming generations of Americans. I suppose your own age might have a bearing on what is being said and what you believe. We still live in a free nation right now, and my prayer is that it will stay that way.

I call myself an ordinary American citizen because of all I have gotten to see and do from the status I have been blessed to serve in. Starting in the cotton fields of West Texas can certainly give you a foundation to be ordinary. After many years of trying to move beyond that particular viewpoint of myself, I worked as hard as I could to elevate myself to a new level of respect and another person's opinion of me. My desire became to be a millionaire and be very recognizable, whether in the workplace or the ministry. It became very hard to go to the ten or twenty-year class reunion and be around all of the classmates who drastically changed their status in life. I was proud of them, but also somewhat jealous. We viewed them by what they had attained in material things, instead of the person we cared for in school. It is amazing how we are segregated because of what we have, instead of who we are personally.

Well, truth be known, I never became a millionaire financially and this was alright with me. I believe God allowed me to look over the crest of the hill to see what I was becoming in trying to attain something that would cost me everything. Some people can handle it, but I guess He saw what was going to be best for my family and myself for the future. Striving so hard for money was leading me into a darkness where I couldn't see through, and was losing my relationship with my children and my wife. I was too dumb and driven to recognize where I was headed in life, until He showed me. I can say with all of my heart, I am so very proud He turned me around. I thought in my mind I was going to do better for my family if I got rich and could provide every need they had, but in reality, I was doing it for my greedy self. I found out all my family wanted was a dad and husband who cared for them more than other things. I made some corrections, and we all became more fulfilled, and with God's grace, we became an ordinary family together again.

## **Please read these verses.**

John 3:16-21 New King James Version (NKJV)

"For God so loved the world that He gave His only begotten Son, that whoever believes in Him should not perish but have everlasting life. For God did not send His Son into the world to condemn the world, but that the world through Him might be saved."

"He who believes in Him is not condemned; but he who does not believe is condemned already, because he has not believed in the name of the only begotten Son of God. And this is the condemnation, that the light has come into the world, and men loved darkness rather than light, because their deeds were evil. For everyone practicing evil hates the light and does not come to the light, lest his deeds should be exposed. But he who does the truth comes to the light, that his deeds may be clearly seen, that they have been done in God."

Jesus was explaining that people condemn themselves when they refuse to believe in God's Son, when they choose the darkness of evil instead of Christ's light of truth. Jesus says very plainly that He was not sent into the world to condemn sinners, but to save them from their sins and give them redemption and eternal life. There is a great life to be lived in the here and now.

America has heard the good news of the Gospel of Jesus Christ over and over, but so many will not believe and continue to walk blindly into the darkness. So many lives are in turmoil and desperation. How can we make a difference and help pull them out of the ruts of life? Anything I say is not a blanket statement that lumps everyone into the same category. We have to decide for ourselves based on what we have heard and believed. Sometimes, as the saying goes, garbage in and garbage comes out. We can curse the darkness, or we can turn on the light! Do we dare look in the mirror and see our nation and our people as we really are? Great question, we will have to answer ourselves.

Writing this book, and as you can tell we did not attack one individual, because this is not our agenda. We believe there is hope for America, and we cannot abandon this nation, which has provided so much for so many, and for many more years to come. So much turmoil is on the horizon if we do not have a change of heart internally. I am praying for a spiritual awakening to come across our nation where lives and Americans will be brought together for the greater purpose. The truth is, America has a heart problem. We should know by now that one human person cannot change the mess we have gotten ourselves into. Not a President can do all that is needed. We must bind together as Christian American citizens and do what we can on our knees in prayer and believe in the power of God to bring the change in the millions of hearts all across this land; from the White House to every house, and to every person who will be willing to get out of our comfort zones and pray and vote.

Psalm 33:12 New King James Version (NKJV)

"Blessed *is* the nation whose God *is* the Lord, The people He has chosen as His own inheritance."

America is still a blessed nation and I believe God still has a great plan for us. My heart will always love and honor this land. Being here now for eighty-two years has given me a brief insight into the freedom, pleasures, changes, and honor we have given each other as a country who believes and honors the God who loves every one of us. When we were formed, He had no one else in mind, so each person is special to Him. Do not forget all that has been given and made available to us and we turn our back on Him; well, allow me to say it this way: may we never, never risk it!! Though the forces of evil are becoming more and more sinister, there is a corresponding cry for a spiritual awakening, not only in America, but also around the world.

I recently read this: "From its inception, our nation's government has been based upon two major tenants: The acknowledgment of a Sovereign God and man's responsibility before God."

May we get back to those two tenants and see all He will do to help bring us back to the place where He gives us guidance, wisdom, faith, love, acceptance, forgiveness, and hope. With God working before us, we can gain back our spiritual influence and commitment. But the people who know their God will display strength and take action. If America will not stand for what is right, she will fall for what is wrong.

Luke 21:25-28 New King James Version (NKJV)

### The Coming of the Son of Man

"And there will be signs in the sun, in the moon, and in the stars; and on the earth distress of nations, with perplexity, the sea

133

and the waves roaring; men's hearts failing them from fear and the expectation of those things which are coming on the earth, for the powers of the heavens will be shaken. Then they will see the Son of Man coming in a cloud with power and great glory. Now when these things begin to happen, **look up** and lift up your heads, because your redemption draws near."

**Consider the following as you seek victory in your personal life:**

1. Be willing to believe all things are possible with God.

    a.  Are you seeking and praying for a miracle in some area right now? Great miracles can happen for you and your family. God certainly wants the best for you as you give Him your life and allow His working power to be active in your heart.

2. a. Is there a robber who is taking the best out of your life right now? We are not talking about a physical being, although that is a possibility. John 10:10 says, *"The thief does not come except to steal, and to kill, and to destroy. I have come that they may have life, and that they may have it more abundantly."* Our enemy, Satan, wants to render us ineffective in our daily walk with Jesus Christ, but he can

only do what we allow him to do because he was defeated by Jesus at the Cross, and the victory was sealed three days later when Christ was resurrected.

3. a. Many of us need to change our mindsets and apply all God has made available in His Word. We walk by faith, not by sight. Constantly fill your mind with the promises of God's love, acceptance, forgiveness, and hope. Always be expecting Him to do great things in your life. It is so easy to get into the negative mindset and have the attitude that you are not good enough to receive what He has promised in the Bible. God gave us His best for our redemption (His Son Jesus Christ), so would He withhold His promises from us because we base our life on our performance instead of faith in Him?

4. a. Recently, I personally went through some illnesses for almost three months. I will be very honest, some doubts started creeping into my thinking. It became very difficult to pray and believe for my healing. My wife is a strong Christian and studies the Bible with intensity. She would pray for me with believer's authority, and my doubts would go away, and the peace of God would come in and replace the thought patterns with hope and belief.

Allow me to share this with you, doubt and unbelief can almost nullify the power of God in your situation, when allowed to enter in. When we enter into the mindset and lifestyle as a believer in Jesus Christ, you stand your ground in Him, regardless of what you see or feel. It's not always easy, but the end result could bring healing and victory in your life.

5. a. Start believing and confessing these words: "I am more than a conqueror" (Romans 8:37). And with Christ in me, "I can do all things through Christ who strengthens me" (Philippians 4:13). Sometimes we need to speak aloud the Word of God and do like the detergent ad that used to be on a television commercial and "Shout it Out." "Greater is He who is in me than He who is in the world" (1 John 4:4), and also, "This is the day the Lord has made. I will rejoice and be glad in it" (Psalms 118:24).

6. a. Did you ever stop and believe that often times a wonderful breakthrough is only one more step forward or just a push away with faith in Christ? WOW, could it be that last effort that breaks open a supernatural possibility we had not seen yet, but have been believing and praying for. Sometimes we pray for years, and when we are about to give up, He shows up and blesses us because of enduring faith in Him. It has been said by many people I know: our attitude determines the heights we will be allowed to go in our work for the kingdom of God. Think on this for a moment, you will only go as high and far as you allow yourself to believe you can go under His leadership and guidance. When He calls and says, "Follow Me," you have a decision

to make and go on into the Promised Land He has in your future. You can always expect His help to come to you and the calling in your destiny, from ways and means you had not seen in the past.

Look for some new possibilities and solutions instead of looking for and being involved in the problems that come knocking all the time.

AMERICANS, TRUST JESUS CHRIST AND HIS WORD AND GET READY FOR SOME MIRACLES IN YOUR LIFE. REMEMBER, GOD'S PEOPLE SEE HIS BIGGER PICTURE IN LIFE. GET ON THE MOUNTAINTOP OF LIFE AND SEE FROM A NEW PANORAMIC VIEW FROM HIS PERSPECTIVE.

# About the Author

J im Jamieson was raised on different farms in West Texas with the family of seven other children. His dad and mother were very hard workers to provide for the large family. The good thing was, everyone old enough had to work and toil in the fields, and this was a very hard life, to say the least. His early life began the mindset of responsibility and a desire to move forward personally and try to achieve and experience the rewards beyond the cotton fields. Being very thankful for his heritage, Jim started looking for the bright lights of his future that could belong to him if he worked hard. There was not a free ride in life, and he knew earning his way would provide some needed satisfaction and self-respect.

Jim did not do very well with his grades in high school. His focus was on other things instead of studying and learning the fundamentals needed for his future plans of achievement. Making failing grades in English and Literature caused a lapse that would be very hard to recover from later in life. Additional discipline was needed in Jim's life; he joined the United States Army and served almost three years in Germany and another year in two military posts in America. Respect was the greatest lesson he learned during his service, which he admits was so beneficial for the future.

Jim became a Christian after the death of their six-year-old son to leukemia in 1972. A few years later, inspiration was given to his heart and mind to develop a television program. Working and learning the computer given to him, the hours, days, and nights finally developed into a program that was shown on stations in America, and opened the doors for patriotic rallies and meetings in many places across our great nation. Remembering the failures in high school, Jim changed his mindset to believe in God's destiny for his life, and started writing articles, which led to writing his first book and having it published in 2014. He gives the complete honor to the Holy Spirit for the completion of this project and the wisdom needed to fulfill this internal desire and dream.

Jim Jamieson has had the great opportunity to pastor for several years, be involved in evangelistic outreach meetings, hosted a Christian television program, served with India Gospel Outreach, and made several trips to India. Jim and his wife, Tillie, traveled extensively across America, holding patriotic rallies and honoring America's military veterans.

He worked as a servant to the Billy Graham Evangelistic organization in 1983 and 1986 in Amsterdam, Holland.

**The additional writers for this book are as follows:**

Chapter 9—Tillie Jamieson writes, "Peace in a Severe Storm." Tillie is the wife of Jim Jamieson, and she has been a beautician for 60 years and still loves doing hair. This is a ministry for her as she touches and helps many lives in various ways. She is a great student of God's Word and teaches on occasions as needed. She has been Jim's wife and great encourager for 59 years. She is a great help to our family as she prays and is with us in the storms of our lives.

Chapter 10—Tina Link writes, "Faith above My Failure." Tina works in the city government and is an awesome asset to her people at work as well. She is a great singer and has taught in a Christian school for several years. Her family is a treasure to her, and she prays for each one for their lives and futures. She also loves the Word of God and communicates and ministers when God opens the opportunity. She is the daughter of Jim and Tillie Jamieson, and a great prayer warrior.

Chapter 11—-Melinda McGlasson writes, "It Isn't about the Struggle, It's about the Victory."

Melinda and her husband Dallas are the pastors of Connection Church in Guymon, Ok. In 2016, she signed as an International Christian Recording artist with Creative Soul Records and McLaughlin Music Group based in Nashville, TN. Her first international album was released in 2016 and is played in 47 different countries. She has had the opportunity to appear on globally televised shows such as TBN and Hour of Power, as well as appearances in various Christian magazines. Melinda also teaches choir in a nearby school system. She is a great worship leader at Connection Church.

Chapter 12—-Fallon Lee writes, "The Beauty of Ashes" She is a current resident of the Dallas, Texas area, a stay-at-home mom to their three beautiful boys, and married to her best friend, Landry. She graduated from Baylor University with a degree in cultural anthropology, with a focus in poverty studies, and now finds her passion in holistic health, nutrition science, home church, pursuing community, and connecting with and ministering to others with chronic illness. She is a great writer; when she has the time to help others who are going through difficult times, she uses this gift of encouragement, as well as many other God-given helps regarding family and friends. Fallon is our grandson's wife and is family to us.

CPSIA information can be obtained
at www.ICGtesting.com
Printed in the USA
FSHW021922011020